THE ART OF REAL ESTATE INVESTMENT

FROM ENTRY TO EXIT

MOTIVATE MEDIA GROUP

PUBLISHED BY:
Motivate Media Group

DUBAI
Media One Tower, Dubai Media City
PO Box 2331, Dubai, UAE
Tel: (+971 4) 427 3000
Fax: (+971 4) 428 2268
books@motivate.ae
www.booksarabia.com

ABU DHABI
Makeen Tower, 9th Street, Al Zahiyah
PO Box 43072, Abu Dhabi, UAE
Tel: (+971 2) 657 3490

RIYADH
Al Hamad Tower, King Fahad Road
Al Olaya, Riyadh
Tel: (+966 11) 834 3595
Fax: (+966 11) 834 3501

LONDON
Acre House, 11/15 William Road,
London NW1 3ER

DIRECTORS: Obaid Humaid Al Tayer, Ian Fairservice
PUBLISHER: Ian Fairservice
GROUP DIRECTOR: Andrew Wingrove
PUBLISHING MANAGER: Vaarunya Bhalla
SENIOR EDITOR: Aswathy Sathish
ART DIRECTOR: Noel de la Pena

ISBN: 978 1 86063 543 4
MEDIA REGULATORY OFFICE APPROVAL NUMBER: MC-02-01-1178936

THE ART OF REAL ESTATE INVESTMENT

FROM ENTRY TO EXIT

FIRAS AL MSADDI

I dedicate this book to the one person who has genuinely inspired me throughout my journey: His Highness Sheikh Mohammed bin Rashid Al Maktoum

PREFACE

I WROTE *The Art of Real Estate Investment: From Entry to Exit* with the aim of helping anyone become a successful real estate investor.

Through this book, I will take you through the basics of the real estate market, why it is such a good investment channel, the dos and don'ts of investing, and how to identify and make the most of opportunities.

It's a journey I have been on myself, and now, as a professional real estate investor and the CEO of one of Dubai's most successful real estate investment companies, I want to share the insights and experiences I have gained along the way.

While I use several examples that focus on Dubai's real estate market, having invested in the UK, France, Turkey, Germany and other GCC countries, I can assure you that the key principles are the same everywhere. Follow them correctly and consistently, and you too can succeed in real estate.

* * * * *

The book starts with an Introduction to my personal journey – a brief look into my childhood and my early days working in sales. I have always felt that I was born to be in sales, and my early years shaped my future and made me determined to be successful. The introduction also talks about my foray into real estate and finding my way in the business, learning through experience, both good and bad.

I have split the rest of the book into four distinct sections. Section One explores the birth and growth of fäm Properties, and how we have become one of Dubai's most successful real estate businesses. Section Two introduces you to the world of real estate investment, and answers questions such as: (1) Why real estate: looking at the many ways real estate represents good investment opportunities;

(2) What to look out for: revealing the inside story of the industry, so you are aware of what to do and what to avoid; and (3) What's next for you: examining whether investment in real estate is right for you.

Section Three is where your own journey begins. The chapters here talk about starting off on the right foot and the basic steps you need to make to start your investment journey; optimising opportunities that would help you make money; and understanding market cycles that would enable you to identify the best times to buy and sell. Section Four details the destination that is success, with: (1) Data or the 'new oil', and why it is crucial for making the right decisions, along with some practical demonstrations which shows the difference it can make; (2) Comparison, or making the right investment by deciding which one, or ones, to go for; and (3) Negotiation and closing, or getting the right deal, which looks at tried and tested negotiating skills and techniques which will make you a winner.

The book closes with an Epilogue, which answers the question, "Where next?", by putting what you've learned into practice, and some guidance on taking up real estate as a professional career. I hope that you not only enjoy reading this book, but also come away with real-life tips and knowledge on how to invest in real estate and become a successful real estate investor.

FIRAS AL MSADDI
FEBRUARY 2022

CONTENTS

"WHY DO THE VAST
MAJORITY FAIL, AND
ONLY A FEW STRIKE
GOLD IN THE WORLD
OF BUSINESS?"

PROLOGUE

REACHING FOR THE STARS

EVERYONE HAS A DREAM – to give their life purpose, meaning and direction. Dreams shape our life choices, give voice to our talents, help build our future and provide us with a sense of control and hope. Not many, however, have the willpower and perseverance to chase their dreams. But if you do, nothing and no one will stop you from reaching the stars.

This is my story in short. From my childhood to my first job as a salesman in Dubai, and through to building a multimillion-dollar group of companies, for which the cornerstone has always been my passion for real estate.

Please join me on my journey as we explore the world of real estate investment with all its ups and downs.

* * * * *

I was born in 1984 in Homs, Syria. I was raised in the city, blessed to be surrounded by a family that gifted me the love and support every child deserves.

As a child, I was highly competitive, with a natural knack for leadership, and I firmly believe that sales has been in my blood ever since my early days. I sold fireworks and toys to the neighbouring kids at a very early age, and when I was 12, I started selling shoes out of a small shop my family owned in Homs. From that point onwards, I dabbled in sales across various markets. I was hooked!

My life-changing moment came one afternoon when I walked into the living room where my brother and mother were watching a show featuring the life coach Dr Salah Al Rashid. He was discussing how people needed to plan in order to achieve their goals. That show changed my life. It inspired me to rethink the way I lived and to dream big. I realised then that my city was too small for my dreams, which led me to leave my home country and explore opportunities abroad.

The plan seemed simple. Move to a different country and pursue bigger goals. But to do that, I needed to be able to communicate effectively in English. With that in mind, I spent that summer brushing up on my language skills with the help of some friends who were visiting from the US.

After studying English for a while, I started applying for jobs. So many interviews! I was even willing to work as security at a shopping mall in Qatar, but fortunately, I was offered a job in sales at a fashion store in Dubai.

On 15 December 2005, I set foot in Dubai for the first time. Little did I know then that this would be where my life would transform forever.

As I was driven to my accommodation in Al Barsha, I remember being awestruck by the magnificent skyscrapers that lined Dubai's famous Sheikh Zayed Road. Something about the city told me that this was a land of opportunities.

Although I'd been practising my English that summer, my fluency probably would have rated at two on a scale of ten. To improve my language skills, rather than living with Syrian friends, I chose to move in with ten Asian guys in a two-bedroom apartment in Bur Dubai. The only way we could communicate was in English!

My life in the retail world had begun. I started at Emporio Armani with an insatiable hunger to learn and progress, which led me to work double shifts – from 9:00 a.m. to 10:00 p.m. – for almost a year, only taking time out to attend evening classes in Business Administration at the Dubai Knowledge Park.

That may seem like a lot of hard work – and it was – but my passion for the job motivated me to do my very best, at every single moment. My determination paid off, as I was selected as the top salesman for Emporio Armani across the UAE. I was rewarded with a black Bulgari watch, which I still cherish.

Nevertheless, despite the recognition, I yearned for something more. The low ceiling for career development in retail had begun to suffocate me, as I had set my dreams and ambitions at a much higher level.

My constant desire for progress urged me to look for different opportunities, and I started applying for jobs and going for interviews again. After over forty failed attempts, the owner of a boutique real estate agency in Dubai Marina offered me a starting position.

With the fixed costs of living in Dubai – and paying for my education – it was quite a risk to leave a secure salaried job and move on to a purely commission-based income, with neither sufficient knowledge about the sector nor proper financial backup. But that didn't stop me from going out on a limb and taking up my first position as a real estate agent, using my twenty-five-day vacation time from the fashion shop.

Dubai Marina was a world within itself. It was like nothing I had seen before. The moment I stepped into the office, I saw ordinary people – people like you and me – living their dream and driving luxurious cars, all from renting and selling properties.

I was immediately convinced that if they could do it, I could do it too. During my twenty-five-day stint, I closed a few rental deals, which gave me the reassurance and confidence boost I had needed to make up my mind. So, I went back to Armani to hand in my notice and start a completely new phase in my life.

It was around this time, towards the end of my first year in Dubai, that another seismic change in my life came about. I met my future wife, who, at the time, was studying at Bristol University and visiting her parents in Dubai for the summer. Just two weeks after we had met, I asked her to marry me, which almost gave her mother a heart attack – it most certainly wasn't the usual British way of doing things! Flash forward to the present, and we have been married for thirteen years. We are parents to two wonderful boys and two adorable girls, and my wife's family have become part of my own. Love will always find a way.

On the other hand, I was taking my first steps in management. After resigning from Armani, I began my new career in real estate. Within a few months, I was approached by a real estate investor I had previously met while I was promoting a property – Mr A. B. Carrim. He approached me with an offer to work for him at his agency, K. C. Real Estate. Within the first few months, I realised that the agency was not working at its full potential, mainly because A. B. – who runs his successful family business conglomerate in South Africa – did not live in Dubai, and the company was not his core business. While I had limited experience in management, I saw the agency's challenges and failings as a lifetime opportunity to enhance my experience by working hard, learning and practising my trade. I firmly believed that I would be able to figure out how to take the company to the next level.

What made me believe that I could turn the business around?

Well, I would say that whatever your business, the recipe for success is the same – and I didn't see it in place at the company, looking at it from the outside. I truly valued the trust A. B. had placed in me and as a result, I was ready to do whatever it took. I had no fear or doubt in my heart whatsoever.

However, a few months down the line, A. B. realised that his financial and time allocations would be better served at home in South Africa and decided to close down the agency. There was a little more time left on the office's lease, so I asked him to give me a chance to revive it. I burned the midnight oil for six months, sleeping in the office several days a week and often working until I zoned out. But I managed to close a few deals for the company, developed a website for them and hired a few agents as well as a receptionist.

A. B. has now become one of our closest family friends – a relationship which started with the trust he placed in me and which I responded to with a hundred per cent dedication to him and his business.

We did well enough to renew the lease, and I managed to sell the company to two investors for AED 1.5 million. I continued as the company's General Manager and was able to grow agent numbers to thirty-five. Unfortunately, the partners had a falling out and became engaged in a legal battle. As I didn't want to get stuck in the ensuing chaos, I decided to move on and join one of the largest real estate developers in Dubai.

However, luck wasn't on my side this time, as I was let go due to the financial crisis that had started in 2007. I tried working for a few other companies, but things were not the same. So, in January 2009, my journey took yet another dramatic new direction.

I made the decision to start what you now know as fäm Properties, and a new chapter of my life began...

SECTION ONE

MY JOURNEY WITH fäm Properties

Success is no accident. It is hard work, perseverance, learning, studying, sacrifice and most of all, love of what you are doing or learning to do.

— PELE

CHAPTER 1

THE BIRTH OF fäm Properties AT THE PEAK OF THE GLOBAL FINANCIAL CRISES

KEY POINTS:

- THE NAME AND THE LOGO
- MAN ON A MISSION
- GROWING AND RELOCATING
- 2013: MY YEAR AWAY FROM fäm
- WORKING FOR A CONGLOMERATE
- NOTHING IS IMPOSSIBLE
- NUMBNESS TOWARDS LIFE
- CONFIDENCE: NATURAL OR EARNED?
- THE FALLOUT AND MY DEPARTURE
- A YEAR OF REPERCUSSIONS
- GROUNDED AND MISSING OUT ON LIFE
- GROWING CLOSER TO GOD AND FAMILY
- PROTECTING MY REPUTATION
- 2015: FINDING MYSELF AGAIN
- LOOKING AT A WORK-LIFE BALANCE
- WHAT DID I GAIN FROM IT ALL?
- NEW PRIORITIES
- DECISION TIME
- GOOD THINGS COME OUT OF CHALLENGING TIMES

AS SOON AS I had made up my mind to go for it on my own, I rented out a shell and core 1,100-square-foot office in Aspect Tower in Dubai's Business Bay. My first rental contract was for three and a half years, and fäm Properties started with just two people – my receptionist Michelle and myself.

THE NAME AND THE LOGO

I still remember that I was not sure what to call my first company. Inspired by some of the largest conglomerates in the UAE, named after the initials of their founders, I decided to call it "fäm", using the initials of my name: Firas Al Msaddi.

The brief I gave my friend who designed the logo was, "I want it to be full of energy, with a corporate and international look and feel," and I believe he did a good job in creating the fäm Properties logo.

MAN ON A MISSION

Although the office space was relatively small, I frosted the glass of my room with the words "fäm Group", despite having no conception of the companies I would be running in the future. I was – and still am – a man on a mission!

Initially, it was just me doing pretty much everything, with Michelle's assistance; HR, listings, marketing, photography and videos, ads, meeting clients, negotiations, contracts and everything else needed at that time – I did the lot.

GROWING AND RELOCATING

Around three years into the business, I was joined by our tech genius, my brother Fateh. We were in a position to hire and train more agents and administrative personnel, so we moved into a larger office space that was 2,200 square feet.

We continued to grow rapidly and within a year and a half we had relocated again, to a 7,000-square-foot office space that I purchased in Bay Square.

2013: MY YEAR AWAY FROM fäm

I was developing into a well-seasoned real estate expert and my growing reputation paved the way for me to have a significant presence in the brokerage industry – to such an extent that I was offered a position as Real Estate Investment Advisor to a very well-known family-owned conglomerate.

I rapidly built my credentials and my track record for delivery at the conglomerate, and within a couple of years, I was asked to operate as Chief Commercial Officer for their entire business. I agreed, not because of the money, but because of my eagerness to explore more, gain experience and increase my market reach and exposure. The responsibility for the daily operations at fäm Properties was placed in the capable hands of my brother, Fateh, who is the COO, and the rest of the team.

WORKING FOR A CONGLOMERATE

Looking back, I believe that 2013 was the breakout year of recovery from 2009's global financial crash. At that time, dedicating all of my time and effort to manage and grow fäm Properties would have actually been far more lucrative. However, that is something I only realised after I ran into serious issues with the conglomerate. It was a world full of bureaucracy and politics, which I had never expected to face, particularly as I had started my own business at an early age and had no real experience of reporting to senior management and dealing with an unpredictable world of corporate politics – all of which comes hand in hand with enterprises of this size and nature. The opportunity to work at that level, however, with all the exposure that it brought, was simply irresistible for someone as addicted to growth and success as I was.

NOTHING IS IMPOSSIBLE

The conglomerate I was working for spanned a wide range of sectors, from real estate development to retail, chartered private jets, helicopters and luxury yachts, trading, oil and gas, and several others.

It was very demanding, but the word "impossible" was never in my vocabulary. I worked harder and harder, day and night – compromising almost every other aspect of my life. I was dreaming big and putting in the hours that would turn my dreams into reality. Or so I thought.

NUMBNESS TOWARDS LIFE

Everything in life comes at a cost. In my case, I call it "the cost of my dreams". The fact that I was overly focused, giving undivided attention to getting my head around my new and challenging role – combined with staying on top of the strategic direction of fäm Properties – led me to becoming totally numb to everything else in my life. I thought about nothing other than progressing in business.

I vividly remember how during the little time off that I took with my family, I was never totally mentally disconnected from work. It took nearly half of my two-week vacation time to even start really "being there" on holiday with them – a direct consequence of my daily work hours from 7:00 a.m. to 11:00 p.m., and the hours spent travelling for work on top of that.

CONFIDENCE: NATURAL OR EARNED?

A question I am often asked is: "Where do you get your confidence from?" This is something I have thought deeply about, and I'd like to share those thoughts. I believe there are two types of confidence.

First is the *natural born* confidence**.** Some people are born with a talent for speaking and acting confidently, despite the level of knowledge they may have about any given topic. I did not fall under this category. I have never been confident speaking about or doing anything that I didn't fully know or understand. Natural confidence, in my opinion, can work to one's advantage when it is backed up by genuine knowledge. Conversely, it can become a serious drawback if not backed up by knowledge and substance.

Secondly, *earned confidence*. This is confidence born from studying, learning and practising whatever you yearn to be confident in. Basically, it is confidence grounded in knowledge and backed up by facts. Confidence in knowing the subject 100 per cent.

This is the source of my confidence when speaking about anything in life, and one of the reasons I always look to gain an in-depth understanding of whatever area I am working in.

THE FALLOUT AND MY DEPARTURE

Toward the turn of the year 2013–14, I started to feel the pressure of problematic political "vibes" between my CEO at the conglomerate and the board. One morning, I arrived at the office to find that the CEO had been replaced with a new successor – and what's more, to discover that he had been forced to leave the organisation on very bad terms with the team as well as with the owners.

Needless to say, I resigned and moved on with my life, concentrating on my own business once again.

A YEAR OF REPERCUSSIONS

After a few weeks had passed, I received a legal letter which led to severe repercussions for me, lasting a whole year while the authorities proceeded with their professional findings.

At this point I must say, I was greatly blessed that such major issues arose in a place like Dubai, where the law always takes precedence over any personal influence. Despite the complexity of the case, it took just a year for me to be given absolute clearance.

GROUNDED AND MISSING OUT ON LIFE

Throughout that time, I was still going into my office at fäm and working, while constantly being dragged down by the negative energy and worrying about "what ifs". But it didn't come without a price. My family had to go on vacation without me because of it, and my kids had to spend time without their daddy. I also missed the wedding of A. B.'s daughter in South Africa, whom I treat like my own.

I went through hell almost every single day and night, not knowing where and how this was going to end. It got to a point where all the money I'd made and the success I had achieved so far came to mean nothing. It was a really hard time to get through.

GROWING CLOSER TO GOD AND FAMILY

I think it's worth mentioning here that this experience made me far closer to God and to my family. During this period, my eldest son had just started school, and it was a wonderful, life-affirming experience to drop him there every morning – something I may not have been able to do if I had continued to work the way I had been previously.

Something else which helped me during this tough time, in addition to my prayers and my wife – who was a great support – was the positivity of my parents. They kept telling me that I would get out of it, which led me to focus more on the fact that I had done nothing wrong. That strengthened my faith and my belief that God would help me through it.

PROTECTING MY REPUTATION

Needless to say, being successful leaves you with a lot of "haters" and unethical competitors who are eager to make the most out of any difficult situation. That's why, trusting my track record and reputation with my main personal investors, I contacted all my clients and told them what was going on.

I was pleasantly surprised, almost overwhelmed, to see them showing their absolute willingness to help me in any way, shape or form. Honesty, integrity and hard work bring their own, rich rewards.

2015: FINDING MYSELF AGAIN

Although I sometimes wish I'd fundamentally changed my approach to work without having to go through such difficult times, those tough experiences made me realise that the merry-go-round of success can come to a halt at any time and for any reason, despite how straight and honest someone is in their life. Why? Because that's just the way it is.

I was pleased with having built a team and a platform at fäm Properties which survived and continued to grow with very little direction or input from me. I went in to work there a few days a week but mostly managed remotely. My experience with the conglomerate changed me to the core.

LOOKING AT A WORK–LIFE BALANCE

Having achieved financial stability and some decent milestones across the fäm Group, I decided that it was time to start looking at my work–life balance. Until today, I believe that if I hadn't endured that dramatic career downturn, I might have carried on with work dominating my life, in a state of unceasing numbness to what should be life's biggest joys. While I did feel lost at times, I managed to flip all the negativity to refuel my determination to break out of it and to start recovering my spirit for life and at work.

WHAT DID I GAIN FROM IT ALL?

So many positives came out of those challenging times. I developed a closer relationship with God and with my family. I also came to know who my true friends are: those who stood by me.

In fact, one of my closest friendships was actually born out of this situation. This amazing friend had a saying that always lifted me up and made me feel better. He expressed it through this story:

A king asked his first advisor to tell him a thought that would make him happy when he was sad, and sad when he was happy. His wise advisor answered, "This too shall pass".

How true that is; whether it's a good time or a bad time, it will always pass and we will always continue to go through ups and downs. I gained other things, too, including a more experienced vision of life, a deeper understanding of what I want and where I want to get to, and an ability to focus on growing my business more than ever before.

NEW PRIORITIES

I made a conscious decision to regard my experience in depth, to look at all I had discovered and to use it to move forward for a better life. I wanted to make sure that what I learned from this experience would be used to improve my way of living and of thinking.

Now, I have reset my priorities in life and I give more time to true friends and the people that matter to me.

DECISION TIME

After a year of struggling, there was one decision left for me to make: do I still continue working and advising my ex-employer on real estate transactions, or not?

The answer was "yes". My logic was that I wanted to continue making substantial deals, so I would have to be dealing with large institutions and influential ultra-high-net-worth individuals anyway. A 100-million-dollar transaction does not happen if you are catering only to ordinary individuals or small businesses. At the same time, it was an opportunity for me to carry on with my head held high – not because of the trauma of my past experiences, but because I truly had nothing to be ashamed of, or to hide. My ex-employers agreed that I had done nothing wrong. I resumed working with them and continue to do so to this day, managing their real estate – but at a business-to-business level and not as part of their conglomerate. They are honorable, good people with whom I continue to take pride in having a healthy relationship.

GOOD THINGS COME OUT OF CHALLENGING TIMES

Realising how wrong I was to join a platform that was not aligned with what I truly aspired to achieve in life was my biggest motive to go all the way in taking fäm Properties and my other businesses to new heights. I never settled for less, and I chose what's been right for myself and my career.

*****

So there you have it. My story so far. It has had its ups and its downs. But I have learned so much, and gained so much. Not just financial success and stability, but an in-depth understanding of the real estate sector – and above all, the true value of things, such as ethics, family, friends, God and work.

Ready to learn more about real estate investment? This book is all about passing on that knowledge and understanding. In the next section, we will look at why real estate can be such a great investment, and the dos and don'ts that can make all the difference to your success. By the time you've read those chapters, you will have developed a real understanding of the immensely lucrative potential of investing in real estate – and you should be ready to decide whether it is for you.

Before we get there, though, the next chapter in this section will provide you with a brief outline of the fäm Group and how it has grown to become such a significant and successful group of companies in the UAE.

CHAPTER 2

THE GROWTH OF THE fäm Group

KEY POINTS:

- BRANCHING OUT INTO NEW VENTURES: HOW WE BUILT THE fäm GROUP

WHEN I DECIDED to take fäm Properties to a new corporate level, I started branching out into new locations. I acquired a couple of new commercial office spaces and rented new retail outlets in areas where we weren't able to buy our own property.

We continue to set new records and expand our business at every level. Early on, as the fäm Group started to grow, we hired a brand strategist to moderate a five-day workshop to identify the DNA of the company – the Why, What, How and When – from which we derived our first CEO message, vision, mission and core values.

We knew who we were and where we were going.

BRANCHING OUT INTO NEW VENTURES: HOW WE BUILT THE fäm GROUP

2009

- The launch of fäm Properties

2014-2016

- Launched **fäm Interiors** with a partner, whom I bought out in 2016.
- Started **fäm Media 24/7**, an outdoor media company, on a 50/50 per cent partnership with the UAE's largest outdoor media supplier.
- Established **fämco Commercial Brokerage** to facilitate rapid marble and construction material trading transactions.
- Launched **fäm Global Properties**, Abu Dhabi.
- Formed **fäm Global Media (outdoor)**, Abu Dhabi.
- Launched **fäm Engineered Snagging and Inspections** for residential and commercial properties.

2016 - 2019

- Launched **fäm Living**, which became one of the largest and most reputable holiday home businesses in the region within just three years. It features over 2 billion dirhams worth of holiday homes under its

management, clustered in the most prestigious areas of Dubai, including City Walk, Downtown, Dubai Marina, Blue Waters Island and Palm Jumeirah, among others.
- **fäm Properties** continued to expand, with new branches and larger offices. We passed the 200-employee mark by the end of 2018.
- At the end of 2018, we celebrated our **tenth anniversary** with the entire team across the fäm Group.
- **fäm Properties** became the number one real estate agency in Dubai, in terms of the number of sales transactions and the value of sales transactions, as recognised by the records of Dubai Land Department, the Government of Dubai.
- Over **3.5 billion dirhams** worth of sales were completed by fäm Properties in 2017 and 2018.

2020 AND BEYOND...

Having exceeded 12 billion dirhams worth of sales across both Dubai and Abu Dhabi, we started 2020 with a collective feeling of success. We were super excited about Expo 2020 Dubai, which was due to open in October. That was, of course, postponed due to the global pandemic. Although 2020 was the year of Covid-19, we continued to expand against all the odds:

- We opened a large office at Dubai Marina and retail branch at Villa Nova Community Centre
- As we continue to grow and expand, more developments and acquisitions are in the planning pipeline across the UAE, China and the UK.

*****

As I am finalising the manuscript of this book, I don't know what the future holds for me, but I do know that my intentions are set in stone. I will continue my personal journey of growth and development, always seeking to improve myself across every aspect of my life. I am determined to continue to share my professional and personal knowledge and experience with the widest audience possible in the humble hope that my message will help better the situation for others too.

Our world is constantly changing, but the fäm Group approach towards conducting business with uncompromising integrity and total client centricity, while empowered by latest technology and data, remains set in stone for myself and the entire fäm team.

HONESTY,
INTEGRITY AND
HARD WORK
BRING THEIR OWN
RICH REWARDS.

SECTION TWO

THE WORLD OF REAL ESTATE INVESTMENT

Real estate cannot be lost or stolen, nor can it be carried away. Purchased with common sense, paid for in full, and managed with reasonable care, it is about the safest investment in the world.

— FRANKLIN D. ROOSEVELT

CHAPTER 3

WHAT MAKES REAL ESTATE SUCH A GREAT INVESTMENT?

KEY POINTS:

- WHY DO THE VAST MAJORITY FAIL, AND ONLY A FEW STRIKE GOLD IN THE WORLD OF BUSINESS?
- THE KEY BENEFITS OF INVESTING IN REAL ESTATE
  - **THE QUANTITATIVE BENEFITS**
    - Security
    - Stability
    - Simplicity
    - Safety
    - Profitability
    - Wealth Preservation
    - Flexibility
    - Capital Gain
    - Leverage
  - **THE QUALITATIVE BENEFITS**
    - Prestige
    - Home Comforts
- THE SIX SECRETS OF SAFE AND SUCCESSFUL INVESTMENT
  - **DIVERSITY IS KEY**
  - **EVALUATE THE RISK**
  - **FIND YOUR PERFECT KNOWLEDGE PARTNER**
  - **COMPARE OPPORTUNITIES AND BE SELECTIVE**
  - **INVEST WITH CONFIDENCE**
  - **DON'T GET CARRIED AWAY WITH SUCCESS**
- WHAT MORE DO YOU NEED TO KNOW?

EVER WONDERED HOW the wealthiest one per cent of the population made their fortunes? You sometimes meet or hear about people who have done extremely well in a particular market. More often than not you – like many others – look up to them. You aspire to be successful like them and to prosper in your own business. If they can do it, then you can too, right? So what goes wrong for so many people? Why do the vast majority fail, and only a few strike gold in the world of business?

The answer is simple. A lot of people invest in ventures they don't completely understand. They make uncalculated and emotional decisions that don't reap any rewards. That may be tough to accept, but sadly, it is the truth.

What can you do, then, if you want to succeed in your chosen business venture? That answer is simple too.

Be cautious and careful, do your homework and make sure you are well informed. Even if a particular market is doing well and is profitable, it can all go downhill if you don't make good choices – and if you don't take the right steps to ensure that your risks are minimised and your potential for profit is maximised.

That's why everything I talk about in this chapter, and throughout this book, emphasises the importance of making well-informed decisions.

Real estate is a market which can bring you enormous financial success – but only if you clearly understand how it works. I know of success stories about people who have established lasting and life-changing wealth by investing in real estate. However, I have also seen some people who have made disastrous, uncalculated decisions without thinking them through – and consequently lost everything.

The point is that when some people follow a hype or trend, they tend to only focus on the good examples and overlook or underplay their risk assessment. But rest assured, in this book, I did not stop at why real estate is such a rewarding investment, I have also shared a lot of practical knowledge on how to assess associated risks and maximise your upside profit potentials.

Before you set out into the world of real estate investment, either as an addition to your profession or trade, as a career, a savvy real estate investor, or simply as a homeowner, you need to remember this most basic principle:

You should only invest in what you can control – and you can only control what you understand.

By the time you reach the end of this chapter, you will have a clear idea about the market, and understand why real estate investment can really reap rewards. You will also see how to invest in what you can control and how to make your investment worthwhile, serving your interests and aims.

THE KEY BENEFITS OF INVESTING IN REAL ESTATE

Before we dive deeper, let's look at the key benefits which make real estate investment such a good idea:

- Security
- Stability
- Simplicity
- Safety
- Profitability
- Wealth preservation
- Flexibility
- Capital gain
- Leverage
- Prestige
- Home comforts

Wherever you are, real estate can be a fantastic investment.

In Dubai, property prices went up from rock bottom in 2009 to *double* the price in 2013. That shows why real estate can be such a fantastic investment. And, as I indicated in the preface to this book, that is true wherever you are investing. Not just in Dubai, but in real estate markets all around the world – as I have found from my own experience.

With the right knowledge about different market cycles and strategies enabling you to identify entry and exit opportunities that maximise your profit, you can be very successful, whatever you invest in.

We'll be looking at that in more depth in Section Three of this book, but right now let's explore the key benefits in the following pages.

First of all, though, a few important points for you to think about:

- Successfully investing in real estate involves doing your homework. Thoroughly and diligently. That's an unavoidable truth.
- You are the one whose money is being invested – so even if you are a client using an agent, you will not succeed without going through the full process of reading, finding, researching, sussing out dishonest people, filtering and qualifying ... doing all it takes to make a well-informed decision.
- A sound investment requires time, money and effort. Making an investment is a major responsibility, and you have to live up to it.

Right, with those points in mind, let's get to those benefits. I'll give you my thoughts on each of them, based on my own experience as an industry insider.

THE QUANTITATIVE BENEFITS

SECURITY

Real estate provides you with the ultimate tangible security. How? Although there are many different kinds of investment, they all come with differing degrees of risk. Thinking rationally, I always start with the one that combines the *least risk* with an acceptable *potential for growth*.

Personally, once I had secured a reasonable portion of my wealth by making low-risk investments, it made sense for me to look into other, more risky, opportunities. How far you go yourself depends on your appetite for risk, your target, budget, cash flow and any other factors that may be specific to you.

Throughout my life, I've made sure that my actions live up to the purpose of setting, planning and achieving my goals.

In real estate, that goal should be to invest in an asset that will not drop dramatically in value, but still offers the potential for great profitability – enabling you to create serious wealth. In this way, it provides the ultimate level of tangible security in our ever-changing world.

STABILITY

Property v Cash: hedging the risk of paper/fiat currency. History has taught us that paper currencies can, and do, sometimes suffer and lose their value. Today, there is much speculation about how much longer "fiat" currencies (government-issued currency that isn't backed by a commodity such as gold) will last, as they are not supported by the gold standard and there are thousands of cryptocurrencies available as possible future alternatives. But, even without that scenario developing, there are considerable risks associated with depending on fiat currency.

Look at the Turkish Lira for instance. In 2012, 1.8 Turkish liras had a value equivalent to 1 US dollar. In January 2020, its value decreased to 7.63 liras for 1 dollar. If you had bought a property worth 1.8 million Turkish liras in 2012, it is maybe today worth around 7.6 million liras – but if you had kept 1.8 million liras in cash, today it would not buy you a quarter of the same property.

This is just one basic example which shows how investing your fiat currency into tangible assets protects your wealth against currency devaluation. There are many more examples – as never-ending printing of currency, sooner or later, leads to its inevitable collapse.

SIMPLICITY

Understanding market fundamentals boosts your confidence. I always say that we invest to prosper, not to bring stress into our lives. One form of stress which can come with investment is if you enter into sophisticated agreements in areas you don't fully understand – be that the rules and regulations or simply the fundamentals.

Your peace of mind and the commercial viability of your investment depends heavily on how much you know and understand about what you are venturing into.

The good news is that real estate is a basic investment most people can understand. The vast majority live under a roof, whether their home is rented or owned. Consequently, property has become a simple investment which does not require a specialist skill-set or education – especially when it is explained clearly, as I hope you will find from reading this book. When you have read it all, you should be able to move into the market with confidence.

SAFETY

Cash flow, passive income and ensuring that your money is working for you safely. Leveraging your cash by deploying a relevant portion of it into safe real estate investment should be an essential part of your lifetime financial game-plan.

When you freeze your money by keeping it in the bank, you miss out on an opportunity for generating cash flow, as that money is not working to its full potential for you. In fact, not only can it also cost money to freeze it nowadays, there are also strong signs of future risk surrounding fiat currency, as I mentioned just now.

During the 2020 coronavirus pandemic lockdowns, many business owners were unable to generate a single penny of profit. Not only that, they also had to inject new capital into their businesses to keep them afloat. One of the very few investment areas that continued to generate passive income was rented real estate, at a time when cash flow was more important than anything else. But investing in real estate, as you will learn in the coming chapters, is not just about generating passive income. It is also about a level of capital gain that no annual bank interest can beat.

PROFITABILITY

Real estate can also generate marginal profit. While unleveraged real estate – that is, fully paid for and without any loans – is one of the safest investments, it can also still offer high marginal profits when it is partially and safely leveraged.

For example, you might buy a property for 1 million dirhams which generates an annual rental income of 50,000 dirhams, translating into 5 per cent gross ROI (return on investment). However, if you buy the same property by taking a 60 per cent loan from the bank (600,000 dirhams) and you inject 40 per cent equity (400,000 dirhams) yourself, your annual rental income of 50,000 dirhams forms 25 per cent gross ROE (return on equity).

When you use the bank's money to invest in real estate, you can increase your returns manyfold. However, you should never overdo it, as that defeats the purpose of investing safely: so do not over-leverage, even if that means generating slightly less income.

If, however, you have a strong risk appetite – which brings with it the potential for much higher profit – you can reinvest your passive income or your capital gains as part-payment for purchasing a new property and use a bank loan to fund the rest of the purchase price, in a way that makes the associated risk affordable.

In other words, if you have just 1 million, don't put it into a real estate investment of 10 million, by adding a bank loan of 9 million. Doing that is risky and defeats the purpose of real estate investment, although it may bring you much more profit during healthy market trends. As they say "higher profit often comes with higher risk". However, if you invested 1 million in a property and in a few years sold it for 1.5 million, depending on your risk appetite, you could risk re-investing 300,000 or 400,000 out of the 500,000 profit on the property you sold – in a highly leveraged real estate deal that could make you many multiples of profit. The associated risk is losing part of, or the majority of, the 300,000 or 400,000 you have invested, but your upside potentials could be multiplying your invested capital by several folds. Meanwhile, your original principal sum of 1 million is kept safe in a fully paid for property.

The point I am trying to make here is that you can take higher risk on part of your profit but never on your original principal capital. I'll be talking more about wise and safe use of bank loans in Chapter 9.

WEALTH PRESERVATION

"Trophy assets" can preserve your wealth. Real estate is also one of the most prestigious or "trophy" assets many people like to own, especially in high-value markets in places like New York, London, Monaco, Paris and Dubai.

Trophy assets may not generate any passive income – in fact, in some circumstances, it can cost money to keep them – but they effectively preserve your wealth. In certain market cycles, they may even offer you the sort of profits you could never imagine.

A good example is how the real estate market across the world and especially in Dubai has reacted in particular; i.e. the ultra luxury segment of real estate that has bounced up more than any other real estate segment.

FLEXIBILITY

Real estate offers geographic diversity. With real estate, you have the flexibility to invest globally according to the strength of the location. If you are a regular business traveller and you have contacts and knowledge in certain cities other than your own, you always have the potential to explore real estate opportunities. They exist everywhere. This offers you the benefit of geographic risk diversity, as the same basic framework for real estate investment applies to most markets.

Flexible forms of ventures based on your strengths and weaknesses. If, like me, your priority is to always play to your strengths while working on overcoming your weaknesses, you'll be glad to know that the flexibility of real estate investment offers you that benefit too:

- If you are an active, energetic investor who can dedicate the time and effort required to read, learn, study, listen, meet, compare and qualify, and conduct site visits, your best form of investment is one over which you can have 100 per cent control – that is to say, sole ownership.
- If you are a less proactive investor, preferring to put your money into something that requires less effort spent on due diligence, management and exit, you can always explore real estate investment opportunities through well-qualified and reputable real estate private equity firms, REITs (Real Estate Investment Trusts) or real estate crowdfunding.
- If you have a limited budget, you can also explore opportunities in real estate through crowdfunding or buying shares in a reputable REIT.
- If you think you have a good eye for design, a passion for decoration or a talent for creating efficient spaces and layouts, you could go in for buying property to furnish, refurbish, rebuild or even build from scratch. When you can unlock the potential value of an existing property by furnishing or refurbishing it, you will always profit from it.
- If you have a passion for building and creating unique living, commercial or retail spaces, you can also monetise your talent for design as a product in its own right. In other words, you don't have to be a contractor or do any physical construction or decorating work – you get third party contractors to execute your ideas and build what you want them to build. You can then sell at a high premium based on the value you have added with your design concept.

CAPITAL GAIN

Real estate provides opportunities for capital gain. While passive income is always your first step, the next level is targeting capital gain – which can be achieved through various strategies:

- Furnish and sell.
- Refurbish and sell.
- Rebuild and sell.
- Build and sell.
- Buy off-plan and sell.
- Buy in low markets and sell in booming markets.
- Identify under-priced properties and resell on margin.

I will elaborate a lot more on the best strategies for targeting capital gain in future chapters.

LEVERAGE

Your real estate investment can be leveraged strategically. Even your exit strategy and exposure can be controlled. So, if you require partial liquidity, you could always seek a refinance loan as long as the risk of your leverage is absolutely under control. That also works well if you need liquidity in a market which does not offer lucrative exit opportunities.

For instance, if the market is down at any given time and you know you will only get a low price if you sell your property, you can refinance with a bank to release some cash liquidity secured against your property, while retaining it to sell during a more buoyant market cycle.

THE QUALITATIVE BENEFITS

Now we have covered the quantifiable benefits of real estate investment, let me share the qualitative benefits as well. These benefits might mean a lot to some people, and nothing to others – but the key point is that in either case, so long as there is an emotional appeal and value for someone, there is a market for it.

PRESTIGE

Social status. Let's take the example of social status in this fast-evolving culture and the era of social media. Some people scoff at social status, but to many, it means the world. So, even if I personally don't care about owning a property which creates or boosts social value for me as an individual, I can still profitably acquire properties in prestigious locations which appeal to people for whom social status is significant. They become my market, so I can invest in the prestigious addresses others dream of … and sell the property, and its status, to them.

HOME COMFORTS

Stability, security and comfort for you and for your family. For me, and for the vast majority of people, it is a fact that we are able to perform better in every way when we are comfortable at home and happy with our family life. Owning your own home offers you and your family the ultimate sense of stability and security – along with, of course, greater security for the future of your children.

Many wealthy people across the world secure homes for their kids next to their own home, so the family ties stay strong and the kids – and their kids – grow up together.

A VALUABLE LESSON I LEARNT ABOUT FAMILY LIFE AND HAPPINESS…

For me, good relationships with the family are most important, and any contribution towards those relationships is immensely valuable. Buying homes for my family and family members works magic in our lives. That's something I learnt a valuable lesson about some years ago…

When I was buying my first land with the aim of building a villa as a home for my family, I spotted a great income-generating investment opportunity while travelling abroad. I decided to substitute building my home in Dubai with this opportunity in a foreign market, as I thought it was a good plan for achieving geographic diversity in my investments. Not to mention the idea that I could use the income from my overseas property investment and maybe rent a bigger house than the home I had intended to build.

When I got back to Dubai, I was really excited about breaking the news to my wife and telling her about this great business opportunity – one which would make our family more money and enable us to diversify our assets.

I will never ever forget her reaction; the sadness of the look on her face shocked me to the core! I was completely caught up in my commercial world of making money and diversifying my investments, so I was bewildered by her reaction. I asked her, "Why are you sad? I can't believe it, you should be so happy for the family!"

She said, "There is nothing like building our own home – a home that will hold our memories of times with our kids and be the cradle of their memories when they are older."

Her reply was an eye-opener for me. I took a step back and thought: "Why am I working so hard? For what? The answer is surely for a happy and comfortable life with my family." Her words had a strong impact on me. I immediately promised her that we would continue building our home in Dubai and that there would never be any change in our family plan for living in that one home. While the details of their own circumstances may differ, I am sure there are many people who can relate to this story.

THE SIX SECRETS OF SAFE AND SUCCESSFUL INVESTMENT

Finally, for this chapter, here are six pieces of practical advice from me. Following them will help to ensure a safe investment which will bring you happiness and prosperity throughout your life.

1. DIVERSITY IS KEY

Depending on your risk appetite, diversify how you use your wealth. This might seem surprising advice from someone whose core business is selling property – but you should always keep a portion of your wealth in cash, despite how promising investment markets can be at times.

Once you have built up a liquid cash foundation, your next step is to look at investing in a sound real estate venture which will bring you rental income and get your money to work for you.

I know many people who have worked hard and saved for years only to use all of that money to buy a property. But I have never agreed with this strategy and never followed it. I prefer to save up money first and create a cash base, then start seeking out investments that will not take up all my cash.

How much should you invest in property? My advice is no less than 25 per cent and no more than 65 per cent of your overall asset portfolio – which includes cash, real estate, gold, business and so on.

2. EVALUATE THE RISK

Once you have decided on your budget, evaluate the risk of any potential investment before looking at the opportunity for profit – even if you are being promised that your capital will be doubled.

I have been a very risk-averse person from the beginning and yet I have still created serious wealth for myself and my clients.

My definition of being risk-averse in this area is that I never enter any investment, despite how attractive it may be, unless:

- I understand what I am doing and I am clear on a) my term of investment and b) my exit strategy.
- Even in the worst-case scenario, my investment will never break the bank for me.

3. FIND YOUR PERFECT KNOWLEDGE PARTNER

No matter how much you try to learn about a market, you can never know it as much as a specialist expert with decades of experience.

It is important to find a "knowledge partner" – an advisor and guide – with all the right qualifications to be by your side.

I'll be telling you more about how to do this, and what to look for, in the next chapter ... so I won't expand upon it here. But hold on to that thought!

4. COMPARE OPPORTUNITIES AND BE SELECTIVE

After evaluating the risk, defining your investment budget and goals – and identifying the right knowledge partner to advise and guide you – the next step is to evaluate the different investment opportunities you have been offered.

You can do this by narrowing your search down to the most appealing offers, then comparing them in order to establish which opportunity provides you with the highest value for your dollar and the maximum profitability.

We'll go into this in more detail in later chapters.

5. INVEST WITH CONFIDENCE

Knowledge is the root of all confidence: ignorance is the root of all doubt and stress.

It is my sincere hope that by the time you finish reading this book, you will have gained all the core knowledge required to start your real estate investment journey – or to enhance the performance of any journey you may have already started.

6. DON'T GET CARRIED AWAY WITH SUCCESS

When you have made good money, in any kind of successful investment – whether in real estate or some other area – going for more becomes very appealing.

But always make sure that you are not tempted to over-leverage your assets. I have seen people make bad decisions on that basis and end up with loans that will take a generation or more to clear. Remember, we are talking about investment – not gambling.

WHAT MORE DO YOU NEED TO KNOW?

What we have talked about in this chapter will hopefully have cleared up most of your doubts about investing in real estate, and how to go about it. However, you may still have some concerns – so let's look at some of the questions I am most often asked...

Q: MANY PEOPLE MAKE MONEY IN THE STOCK MARKET WITHOUT UNDERSTANDING IT. SO WHY CAN'T I?

FIRAS: Many also lose their lifetime savings. The risks are simply not worth it, especially if you are investing in stock markets before you've secured some tangible investment in real estate. Stock market investment is beyond your control. It often lacks consistent, fundamental principles or is driven by factors you cannot understand unless you are an expert. It is impacted by way too many moveable and transient influences, not just basic commercial ones.

Q: ISN'T THE STOCK MARKET A MORE LIQUID INVESTMENT?

FIRAS: Do you want to invest so you can cash out or do you want to invest to establish a secure source of income and pave the way for capital appreciation opportunities? It is easy to cash out, but making a profit or a loss is out of your control. What's more, in extreme down market positions (such as the 2009 financial crisis), liquidation can be prevented by law!

Q: IF YOU DON'T UNDERSTAND OTHER INVESTMENT OPTIONS, HOW CAN YOU COMPARE THEM?

FIRAS: Understanding the principles of a market helps us come to a conclusion about what is right or wrong for us. So, if someone knows the stock market better than real estate, then for sure, the stock market is their first option and real estate becomes their second one.

Q: TRUE OR FALSE? MANY PEOPLE SAY THAT BUYING A HOME FOR YOURSELF IS A LIABILITY. THEY SAY IT'S BETTER TO BUY PROPERTY TO RENT OUT FOR INCOME INSTEAD.

FIRAS: There is no right and wrong answer here. For some, buying a home for their family means the world, while for some others, the emotional value of owning their own home does not mean much. So they might rent a house to live in and invest their cash in income-generating properties. It is really a personal decision, with no set rules or a single correct answer.

You need to do what feels right for you. The family story I told you a little earlier is a perfect example of this. For my wife, it was not about investing abroad, investment diversity and renting a bigger house in Dubai. It was about owning and settling down in what we could call a family home that would hold our cherished family memories and our best moments together.

Q: PRICES CAN DROP IN REAL ESTATE, CAN'T THEY?

FIRAS: True. But unlike some other investments we all know that, historically, property prices keep increasing in the long-term despite the ups and downs. What's more, they will never drop to zero. What could be better than an investment you know cannot go wrong in the long-term despite any short term price and market fluctuations? It is one of the very best investments I can think of – one that provides you with a controlled level of risk.

The first rule for any investment I make is: Can I measure the risk, and more importantly, can I afford the risk if the worst-case scenario occurs? Then I look at the potential for rental income and capital gain. For me, investing in real estate is a winner.

*****

Now that we have looked at the benefits of investing in real estate, I hope you can see the great potential it holds for you. In the next chapter, I will reveal the untold story of real estate, the tricks of the trade and the traps and hurdles you'll need to look out for, as you set out on your own investment journey.

CHAPTER 4

REAL ESTATE: THE INSIDE STORY, REVEALED

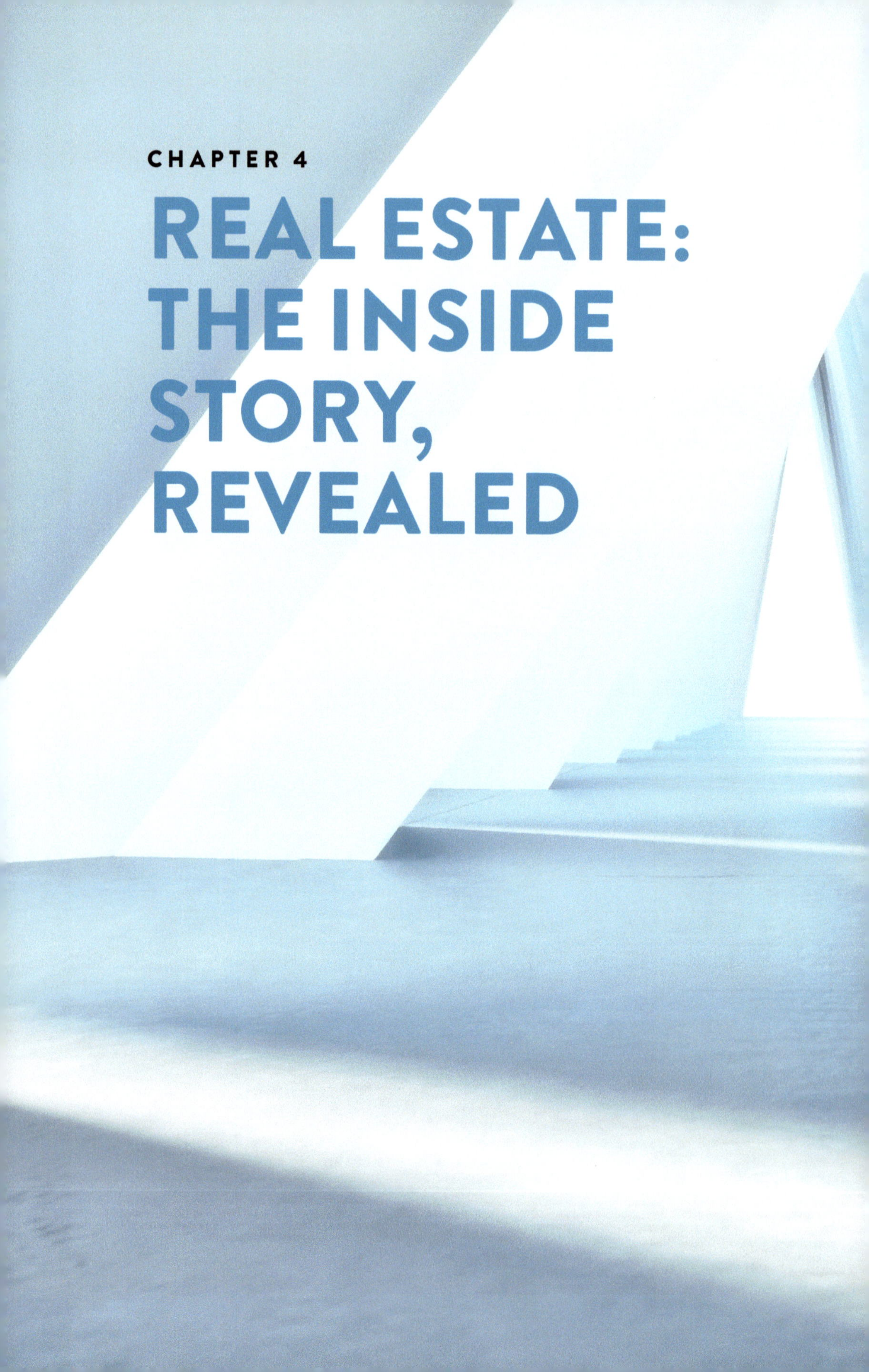

KEY POINTS:

- KNOWING THE DOS AND DON'TS
- WHY YOU NEED TO KNOW WHAT'S REALLY GOING ON?
- SAY "NO" TO THE NEGATIVES
- WHAT DO YOU NEED TO KNOW BEFORE INVESTING?
- KNOWLEDGE PARTNERS
    - **THE IMPORTANCE OF FINDING THE RIGHT "KNOWLEDGE PARTNER"**
    - **WHAT WILL A KNOWLEDGE PARTNER DO FOR YOU?**
    - **WHAT ARE THE QUALITIES TO LOOK FOR IN A "KNOWLEDGE PARTNER"?**

REAL ESTATE IS A HUGE industry, with many tales to tell – tales that might inspire, motivate, surprise or even shock you, as well as enlighten you. But like every industry, this also has two sides. The first is the story that most clients and customers know. The second is a story that only the inside players and service providers are aware of. This is that story...

Most, if not all, real estate investment books talk about the wonderful benefits of investing in real estate – and it is indeed true that real estate is probably the best investment you can make, as we talked about in the previous chapter.

But even what looks like the best investment venture can end up producing unwanted and costly results when it is done badly or incorrectly, or if the investor falls foul of the "tricks of the trade". Before you begin to invest, I want to inform you of the wrong or "dodgy" practices you need to be aware of and avoid.

Naturally, it can be a bit daunting for clients to read about what really goes on in real estate investment – the nitty-gritty or its "inside story".

But that inside story delivers invaluable insights to the investor who wants to be in the know and in tune with the industry – with their brains hot-wired into being amongst the first to identify opportunities, as they have more knowledge than most.

In this chapter, I'd like to offer you some advice based on my experience. Put into practice, this advice can be monetised to an extent you might never have imagined.

KNOWING THE DOS AND DON'TS

To make successful real estate investments, you need to know the ropes and understand both the dos and the don'ts of the industry. If you are not familiar with what you should go after and what you should avoid, you are going to be in for some surprises – many of which could be unpleasant and cost you money. You are investing to *make* money, so you certainly don't want to *lose* what you've already put in, do you!

So, before learning about real estate investment in more detail, which you will in the later sections of this book, I believe it is vitally important for you to be aware of the most common mistakes many investors make ... along with the most common false promises and risky structures some real estate advisors push on to their clients, simply for the sake of pocketing easy commissions.

WHY YOU NEED TO KNOW WHAT'S REALLY GOING ON?

It's an unfortunate fact (but fortunate for you!) that the vast majority of people intending to invest are more interested in admiring alluring lifestyle images and slogans than engaging with informative and enlightening facts and data. In fact, I'd say that as few as two out of a hundred take the latter approach.

That presents a fantastic opportunity for the investor who is prepared to do their due diligence and study the market well before making their first move into the marketplace. It puts them in the pole position for seeing and seizing the best opportunities – and avoiding the costly perils and pitfalls.

SAY "NO" TO THE NEGATIVES

When you have the right information and knowledge at hand prior to getting involved, you'll be wised up enough to evade a whole catalogue of dangers like:

- X Losing your money on property speculation or by following wrong practices.

- X Taking out high financial leverage, beyond what you can afford.

- X Using bank money (property mortgages) during risky market cycles.

- X Falling for "guaranteed rental income" scams.
- X Signing biased legal contracts concerning your real estate purchases.
- X The risks of dealing with a chain of real estate agents.
- X Overpaying and/or being misled on what are fair market prices.
- X Following manipulated price evaluation reports and market reports.
- X Missing out on serious investment opportunities by following other over-promising offers.
- X Starting your negotiations on the wrong foot with sellers and tenants.
- X Not understanding the final net profit/ income on your real estate investment.
- X Failing to identify the right real estate consultant/knowledge partner for you – someone experienced, knowledgeable and ethical, whom you can trust.
- X Missing out on calculating and factoring in fixed costs and ongoing expenses not mentioned in the sales talk.
- X Not understanding your exit options well.
- X Failing to maximise your profit and minimise your risk.

WHAT DO YOU NEED TO KNOW BEFORE INVESTING?

There are many factors you should be mindful of before going through with any investment decision – including the over-promises and common myths some developers and real estate agents, driven purely by profit and commission, might use to lure you into investing in their properties.

Whether you are investing in properties in off-plan projects, properties on the resale market, real estate crowdfunding or via private equity real estate firms, there are many "sharp practices" you need to be aware of and avoid.

You will often come across real estate advisors promoting various offers to secure a sale for themselves, including the following approaches discussed here.

As an active real estate investor who has invested in different parts of the world, I have been exposed to many offers or situations that I managed to avoid, and which I would advise you to avoid as well. These kinds of scenarios can happen irrespective of how mature the market you are investing in is. Hence you have to be self-aware.

Encouraging you to buy an off-plan property on a payment plan with the aim of placing a down payment now and selling before the next payment comes due. This defeats the purpose of investing in real estate. As mentioned in the previous chapter, one of the best aspects of such investments is the high level of safety, security and steady income they can offer. Short term investment in real estate should never be your primary strategy or plan A.

Although it is indeed possible to resell a property after making the first or partial payment, hence multiplying your invested capital by many folds, you should never buy an off-plan property unless you are certain that you can afford to make all future payments. If a profitable exit appears earlier, then you could capitalise on it and cash out your profit.

Getting you to pay a large sum of money for a premium view that will sooner or later be blocked by another building. It is crucial to always look at the surrounding plots and neighbouring areas around the project you intend to invest in. I know of many cases where investors paid high premiums to secure the best views from their apartments, which were soon blocked by other projects. So, don't just take the salesman's word for it ... always seek a reliable reference, preferably from the zoning authority of that community or – even better – from a governmental body, where applicable.

Trying to get you to buy leftover apartments packaged as highly attractive, special and limited offers. The lowest-priced property in the project does not necessarily offer the best investment opportunity. Do your homework and always look for genuine value, not so-called "bargain" offers.

Getting you to sign your legal SPA (Sales and Purchase Agreement) without giving you a chance to read it – telling you it is a standard document you need not worry about. What you sign for is what you have to comply with from that moment onwards. The salesman who led you through the process may not even be there for you in the future. So, ensure that you read the commercial terms of your contracts thoroughly to be 100 per cent certain that they're in line with your own investment figures. Once you've done that, pass the contract and your own commercial brief to a lawyer to ensure that the commercial framework you are accepting is legally defined in your contract of sales. A word of caution, though: lawyers can advise on legal matters but often don't have the experience to provide you with sound advice on commercial terms. In some cases, they might even provide you with legal advice that totally defeats your commercial purpose. You absolutely must ensure that your precise commercial brief is provided to your legal advisor or solicitor from day one.

Telling you that you don't need to commission a professional snagging inspection for the property, especially when it is brand new – or even telling you that you can snag and inspect the property yourself. Whether new or previously occupied, one of the basic ABCs of acquiring a property is to inspect it and ensure that there will be no costly surprises in the future. If you simply make a shallow visual inspection, you are likely to overlook possible faults behind the ceilings and walls and/or plumbing or air conditioning issues. You must engage a professional property inspector to do this job for you.

Camouflaging costs that are vaguely mentioned in your contract of sale and purchase. Sometimes, you might read a comprehensively detailed table of figures and costs involved in a property purchase and be satisfied with it. Beware! You could miss the one line that states that the seller has the right to charge you extra, change certain charges in the future, or something similar. So, make sure that you read it thoroughly and are 100 per cent clear and certain about every single confirmed and possible future charge related to your purchase.

Luring you with offers like "Buy an apartment and get a car with it". I would like to believe that it is clear to the vast majority that special offers which come with cars, expensive gifts and so on are definitely *NOT* free of charge. Any cost associated with the sales is already built into the price you are paying for the property. Unfortunately, though, I have seen many investors buy overpriced properties after being tempted by some sort of prize, special offer or freebie. As a result, they made massive losses when they wanted to resell – not because the market was poor, but because the properties they bought were overpriced to start with.

Fancy sounding titles for real estate salespeople. Many salespeople go under fancy labels such as property investment advisors, real estate investment experts and so on

– which can often impact the way investors perceive and trust the advice they offer. I am not saying that *all* of them don't live up to or deserve their titles, but unfortunately, a *lot* of them don't. It is important that investors check and appraise how qualified their property advisors are to sell and offer real estate investment opportunities.

Your advisor should be chosen extremely carefully. When you identify the right one, you should have an indispensable "knowledge partner" whom you can trust to advise and guide you at every stage. I'll be telling you more about how to achieve this at the end of this chapter and in Section Three.

Real estate agents getting kickbacks from sellers on properties offered on the resale market. This is something you need to keep in mind to avoid any hidden agendas property salespeople may have planned in cahoots with property sellers.

Always include a clause in your Sales and Purchase Agreement (SPA) stating that the broker/agent, the buyer and the seller have explicitly stated all their rights to receive any payments or fees and that there are no side agreements between any of the parties, other than what is stated in your contract of sales and purchase.

Having buyers subject to finance approval. If you are selling your property, be mindful whether it is an unconditionally binding sale or is subject to certain milestones. For instance, the sales agreement being subject to the buyer obtaining finance approval from their bank. Sometimes these conditions can be overlooked by sellers, as the entire contract seems to be fully aligned with their mutual agreement – but there is a single line stating something like "this contract is subject to the buyer obtaining finance approval from the bank".

Even if that is the case, it might still be okay, provided that it is time-limited, and that the seller is fully aware and has factored it when planning their cash flow in case the transaction has to be cancelled due to the failure of the buyer to obtain finance approval. The sales agreement can be subject to a number of similar scenarios. We've mentioned finance, but it can also be related to inspecting the property. Always read and be fully aware of the small print and conditions.

Property that comes with "issues". When buying a used property which is relatively old, it is essential to engage a property inspector to generate a snagging report before you sign up to any binding Sales and Purchase Agreement with the seller. You don't want to invest in a property that becomes a major liability due to serious maintenance or even structural issues.

Subleased property. Buying subleased property is never recommended, unless you engage a very good legal advisor to review every detail of the lease. You need to be fully aware that you will inherit any and all rights, liabilities and risks associated with the subleased property. Moreover, when properties are subleased, the landlord basically has no binding leasing agreement with the actual occupier of the property.

The landlord's tenancy binding agreement is with the first tenant who – if they face any financial problems or decide to leave the country for any reason – could present problems. It will be a lengthy process legally dealing with the occupier, who may have paid the rent upfront to the lead tenant.

So, if you are buying a tenanted property, you can always request to meet with the tenant by way of introduction. Or you can mention in your sales and purchase contract that the property would not be sub-leased.

Paying your security deposit or down payment directly to the seller's account and not to your escrow agent. It is essential that your down payment or security deposit is held in the custody of a third-party agent (a buyer's agent) or an escrow agent. Vice versa if you are the seller; your payment or security deposit has to be held in the custody of a third party and not the buyer.

*****

Everything I've talked about in this chapter is based on real life stories and situations I have encountered. To look on the positive side, I see lots of people making healthy annual returns and enjoying high profits on their real estate investment. But there are definitely perils and false promises to watch out for when investing in real estate.

For instance, I have met investors who are not happy with their annual service charges, because they did not read their Sales and Purchase Agreement or may have read it but without paying close attention to charges on their investment plan.

Then there are the investors who bought crazily overpriced units from developers who focus their sales patter on new buyers and not on repeat buyers. If they had simply checked the prices by going onto a mobile app or website (that shares information on government data for registered sales transactions, or shares data on property evaluation) or spoken to other reliable real estate agents selling in neighbouring projects, they would have been able to make a more informed decision.

That's why I cannot emphasise enough the fact that it's all about doing your homework.

All this information I've provided you with might have given you a great insight into what to do, and what not to do. But you may still want to ask me, "Others have made so much money purely by speculating, without doing all this research. Why can't I?"

Well, I would compare this to a sheer stroke of luck. It is exactly like saying, "What about those few who made so much money winning the lottery?" Just remember, the operative word in that question is *few*.

So, when you begin investing in real estate, make sure that you are not speculating blindly for a quick profit. Aim for medium- to long-term investment instead and enjoy any earlier short-term results if they should come along.

But if you *still* wish to speculate, despite my advice, then the best advice I can give you is to only take well-calculated risks. The same way you are motivated by the very best possible high profit margin, factor in the worst-case scenario – and ensure that if it does happen, it won't break your back.

Here are a few more words of advice before we move on... Always investigate the location of the project and do your research on the surrounding plots to ensure that the view you paid for will not be lost in the future. There's an anonymous saying which is so apt in this context: "Buildings don't move, but neighbourhoods change all the time". So be careful!

Last, but not least, keep your eyes on the prize. Please don't be intimidated or demotivated by the "don't dos" mentioned in this chapter, because knowing what you should and shouldn't do when investing will make that investment bulletproof – and will enable you to join the ranks of those who have created and multiplied their fortunes manyfold by investing wisely in the real estate market.

By now, I hope that you have a deeper knowledge about the world of real estate and the sometimes-harsh truths that dwell within it. In the next chapter, we'll be looking at different ways of investing. But first of all, here's that information about "knowledge partners".

KNOWLEDGE PARTNERS

THE IMPORTANCE OF FINDING THE RIGHT "KNOWLEDGE PARTNER"

Why is having a "knowledge partner" so important? Well, let me remind you of a few points I made in the last chapter:

- You should only invest in what you can control – and you can only control what you understand.

- With the right knowledge about different market cycles and strategies enabling you to maximise your profit, you can be successful, whatever you invest in.
- Successfully investing in real estate involves doing your homework. Thoroughly and diligently. That's an unavoidable truth.

Understanding. Knowledge. Homework. They are all vital to your success – and to avoiding the pitfalls I have talked about in this chapter.

Here's something else I said earlier: *No matter how much you try to learn about a market, you can never know it as much as a specialist expert with decades of experience.*

This book is designed to help you become a real success in real estate, and to help you make the right decisions. But you won't become an expert overnight, so it's essential that you find the right knowledge partner to be your adviser and guide. Someone who is an old hand at the business and knows the ropes – and someone you know you can trust, of course.

WHAT WILL A KNOWLEDGE PARTNER DO FOR YOU?

Being a success is all about maximising the opportunities offered to you by investment in real estate.

You *benefit* from an opportunity when you're the first to see and seize it and you *maximise* the benefits when you capture it correctly and at the right time. So, if you identify an opportunity and go for it, you reap the benefit.

However, if you choose the right knowledge partner to negotiate the commercial terms for that opportunity, you will most likely maximise the benefits and also minimise the risk.

For instance, you could decide to invest 1 million in a particular property directly from the developer because you know there is a good investment opportunity in it: the timing is right, the market cycle is right, the location is right, and the quality is right.

However, an expert who knows not only this particular developer, but also has an all-round understanding of most developers and has worked with real estate investors and first-time homebuyers for many years – and so has a great understanding of the entire journey before and after signing the investment contract – can advise you on how to negotiate aspects of the contract to avoid potential obstacles and perhaps even replace them with benefits.

Here are few examples:

- A seasoned real estate expert with a proven historical track record understands exactly the bottom price or the best offer a particular developer has ever sold at. So, yes, it may be a really good opportunity to buy at 1 million – but what if you could actually achieve 950,000? An experienced real estate expert knows the bottom line and can, therefore, direct your negotiations.
- A seasoned expert may have developed great relationships with key senior decision makers in the market and therefore have an insight into any new or upcoming rules and regulations which might be likely – and which could impact your investment up or down. It could be, for instance, right to buy today, but not tomorrow, if you know that higher registration or stamped duty fees will be announced tomorrow. Or the other way around.
- Most individual real estate investors might not know that the handover day can be two to three months away from moving in or from actually receiving the keys. Handover might even be four months from being able to move into the property if many defaults or snags had to be fixed by the developer. A seasoned knowledge partner will advise you on how to overcome that at the time of signing the Sales and Purchase Agreement with the real estate developer.

WHAT ARE THE QUALITIES TO LOOK FOR IN A "KNOWLEDGE PARTNER"?

Many people don't see much value in dealing with a middleman or broker – in our industry, a real estate agent. In fact, some tend to find ways to circumvent middlemen, but for me, the right person will become your "knowledge partner" who can help you in numerous ways, as shown in the examples in the previous page.

So, what should you be looking for when identifying a knowledge partner? They should be someone who:

- Knows the inside story about forthcoming rules, regulations, projects and city planning.
- Follows a consultative sales approach grounded in market fundamentals, data and statistics.
- Depends less on brochures and lifestyle images to sell.
- Is client-centric in every way, shape and form.
- Has a proven track record, which you can check through client testimonials and reviews.
- Utilises technology to create more value.
- Knows the entire range of products within his/her market.
- Knows current and historical market trends and has a proven ability to "read" them.
- Mostly works on success fees only.

I'll go into the process of identifying the right partner in greater depth later in this book, but first of all, I'd like to tackle a common misconception about real estate agents and their suitability as knowledge partners.

More often than not, there is a trust deficit between agents and customers. In 2014, when I wrote the CEO message for my company, I stated, "Real estate agents are often the pariahs everyone loves to hate." However, I took this as an opportunity for me at fäm Properties to build an uncompromising value system. I work assiduously to embed this value system into every team member so that they become worthy of being trusted as knowledge partners.

Whether we are talking about doctors, engineers, lawyers, teachers or real estate agents, you will always find the poor, the average and the excellent. It is your job to do what it takes to identify the excellent – and that's something we'll be covering in Chapter 7.

After all, if the right – the excellent – real estate agent is not your knowledge partner, then who is?

- Is it you? We have already established that, logically, an average investor cannot have the expertise of an agent with years of experience.
- If not you, then whom? Is it the salesman at the developer's office? Like I've mentioned before, all salespeople at developers' offices have a single mandate – which is to exclusively sell their company's properties with all its good, average and least attractive units.
- Is it your banker, who is engaged in banking work throughout the week?
- Or is it any agent?

My answer would be "none of the above". There is only one way to maximise the outcome of your investment decision and that is by leveraging the experience of the right real estate agent. And this can be achieved only if you invest time and effort in finding the right individual. When you do, you will have identified an invaluable partner – someone you can trust and depend on at every stage ... as many of my clients do with me, and with my team.

CHAPTER 5

THE FIVE MAIN REAL ESTATE SEGMENTS TO INVEST IN

KEY POINTS:

- WHICH TYPE OF REAL ESTATE INVESTMENT IS RIGHT FOR YOU?
    - **1. BUYING A HOME FOR YOURSELF AND/OR YOUR FAMILY**
    - **2. BUYING TO GENERATE RENTAL INCOME**
    - **3. BUYING TO RESELL WITH PROFIT**
    - **4. CORPORATE INVESTMENT**
    - **5. PROFESSIONAL INVESTMENT**
- WHEN IS IT TOO EARLY OR EVEN WRONG FOR YOU TO INVEST IN REAL ESTATE?
- INTERESTED IN A CAREER IN REAL ESTATE INVESTMENT?

WHICH TYPE OF REAL ESTATE INVESTMENT IS RIGHT FOR YOU?

By now, you will have a broad but clear insight into what a rewarding and profitable investment real estate can be, and you will be familiar with the basic dos and don'ts.

Remember, the same principles apply wherever you are investing. From Dubai to Dublin and from New Zealand to New York, the real estate sector primarily operates under the same basic principles.

The next essential step is defining the purpose of your investment. This will help you to start your journey on the right footing and, ultimately, to achieve your aims. So which type of real estate investment suits your life, your needs and your preferences?

Broadly speaking there are five categories of real estate investment you might consider: (1) Buying a home for yourself and/or your family – although your direct intention or motive to buy a home is not to invest but to live in, it is still considered as a valuable real estate investment; (2) Buying to generate rental income; (3) Buying to resell with profit; (4) Corporate investment, i.e. buying to expand your business; and (5) Professional investment, i.e. buying, renting and selling, or even buying land to develop with the aim of creating your rental income portfolio or with the objective of reselling, targeting capital gain.

Whichever category you might fall into, there are some important questions you need to ask yourself so that you can make an informed, intelligent and achievable decision.

Take some time to sit down and make a list of your wishes and options based on the questions I have suggested in the following pages. Spending some time now establishing exactly what you want and what is possible could be one of the wisest investments you'll ever make for your future...

1. BUYING A HOME FOR YOURSELF AND/OR YOUR FAMILY

The first rule; whether you are intending to live in it or not, buying a real estate asset has to be treated and dealt with as one of the most substantial investments an individual can make either way. Investing in a place to live in is more than just about being where you want to be...decorating it the way you want, for instance, not having to stress about moving between rented houses every few years, creating a home to hold your precious family memories and providing a sense of assurance and security for your family - important considerations though those are of course.

It is also a sound and sensible alternative to paying rent elsewhere. A way of not only preserving your wealth, but also benefiting from potential capital appreciation for sale or to leave as a legacy.

If this is what you are looking for, here are some questions you should ask yourself:

WHAT ARE THE KEY ESSENTIALS THAT THE PROPERTY MUST HAVE AND WHICH YOU ARE NOT PREPARED TO COMPROMISE ON? EXAMPLES INCLUDE SIZE, BALCONY, TERRACE, VIEW, GARDEN, POOL, PRIVACY, SUNLIGHT, PROXIMITY TO SHOPS, SCHOOLS, COLLEGES AND UNIVERSITIES, TRANSPORT LINKS, BEACHES, MOUNTAINS – THE LIST WILL BE DIFFERENT FOR EVERYONE.

WHAT IS YOUR BUDGET? WHAT CAN YOU REALISTICALLY AFFORD WITHOUT STRETCHING YOUR FINANCES BEYOND SENSIBLE BOUNDARIES?

MORTGAGE OR CASH? HOW DO YOU WANT TO BUY - SPREADING THE COST OVER A PERIOD OF YEARS WITH A MORTGAGE OR PAYING IN CASH, EITHER IN FULL OR PARTLY?

- HOW COMFORTABLE ARE YOU WITH THE LEVEL OF MORTGAGE PAYMENTS? HAVE YOU THOROUGHLY PLANNED YOUR CASH FLOW AND REPAYMENTS?

- AFFORDABILITY: DOES YOUR BUDGET ENABLE YOU TO BUY YOU A HOME WITH ALL YOUR ESSENTIAL PREFERENCES - AS ESTABLISHED IN POINT 1? OR WILL YOU NEED TO RECONSIDER SOME OF YOUR PRIORITIES?

- WHAT IS YOUR TIME FRAME FOR MOVING IN? IS YOUR NEED, OR WISH, TO MOVE URGENT AND IMMEDIATE - OR CAN YOU WAIT AND WATCH THE MARKET UNTIL THE RIGHT PROPERTY COMES ALONG, AT THE RIGHT PRICE?

- IS IT GOING TO BE A 'HOME FOR LIFE'? ARE YOU PLANNING TO SETTLE DOWN NOW IN THE HOME YOU WANT TO SPEND THE REST OF YOUR DAYS IN, OR IS THIS A STEP OR STAGE IN YOUR HOME-OWNING JOURNEY - WITH A PLAN TO MOVE ON AS YOUR LIFE PROGRESSES OR YOU NEED TO RELOCATE?

- ARE YOU FACTORING IN YOUR FAMILY'S LIFE CYCLE OVER THE COMING 10 YEARS? YOU COULD BE A YOUNG COUPLE AIMING TO START A FAMILY, OR YOU COULD ALREADY HAVE A LARGE FAMILY BUT WITH CHILDREN OF DIFFERENT AGES WHO MAY BE OFF TO COLLEGE, ABOUT TO GET MARRIED THEMSELVES, TAKING UP CAREERS ELSEWHERE - OR STAYING AT HOME FOR THE IMMEDIATE FUTURE. THEY'RE ALL KEY FACTORS IN CHOOSING THE SIZE AND LOCATION OF YOUR HOME, AND THE COMMITMENT YOU MAKE TO IT.

- WHAT ABOUT RESALE VALUE? IF YOU'RE NOT PLANNING TO LIVE IN YOUR NEW HOME FOR A

LONG PERIOD, PERHAPS EVEN THE REST OF YOUR LIFE, WILL IT APPRECIATE ENOUGH IN VALUE TO ENABLE YOU TO MAKE THE NEXT MOVE YOU ASPIRE TO?

WHAT SORT OF PROPERTY IS BEST FOR YOU, TICKING OFF ALL YOUR REQUIREMENTS? READY TO BUY AND MOVE INTO, NEW OR IN A PROPERTY CHAIN, OFF-PLAN, UNDER CONSTRUCTION...OR WOULD IT BE BEST TO BUY A PLOT OF LAND AND BUILD ON IT, TO YOUR OWN DESIGN AND PREFERENCES?

2. BUYING TO GENERATE RENTAL INCOME

You might be investing this way as a long-term or a medium-term rental project, possibly by buying or building a property to let out on either a short-term or annual basis. Some people who do this may intend to live in the property eventually, but want to rent it out in the meantime. Buy to let property is also sometimes used as a holiday or second home, which is rented out for the rest of the year when not used by the owner.

Either way, it can provide regular income whilst also being a capital asset which grows in value. As time goes by, many of these landlords realise a decent level of capital gains.

This kind of investment applies to both residential and commercial properties. Purchasing commercial assets, offices or retail outlets that are then rented on a long-term basis to blue-chip corporates is a very popular buy to let investment across the world.

You have a number of options to choose from if you are buying to let: it can be a direct investment where you are the sole owner of the property you rent out, or you can co-invest with others - for instance with a real estate crowdfunding investment company or with a real estate private equity investment organisation.

If you are considering buying to rent out, see the questions you need to ask yourself on the next page:

- WHAT IS YOUR BUDGET? WHAT LEVEL OF INVESTMENT CAN YOU SENSIBLY AFFORD TO MAKE?

- WHAT ARE YOUR KEY PREFERENCES? A RENTED AND MANAGED PROPERTY, OR A LOCATION CLOSE TO WHERE YOU LIVE OR WORK AS YOU KNOW THE AREA AND IT IS EASY FOR YOU TO MANAGE IT YOURSELF?

- MORTGAGE OR CASH? ARE YOU GOING TO TAKE OUT A MORTGAGE TO PAY FOR THE PROPERTY, OR PAY CASH?

- DO YOU WANT TO BUY A PROPERTY THAT IS ALREADY RENTED OUT, ONE THAT'S VACANT BUT READY TO BE RENTED - OR A PLOT OF LAND ON WHICH TO BUILD A PROPERTY AND RENT IT OUT?

- WHAT LEVEL OF RETURN ARE YOU EXPECTING IN TERMS OF RENT FROM YOUR TENANT/S?

- WILL THE EXPECTED RENTAL INCOME COVER YOUR MORTGAGE PAYMENTS OR JUSTIFY YOUR CASH EXPENDITURE?

- MANAGEMENT: ARE YOU GOING TO MANAGE IT YOURSELF? OR WILL YOU NEED TO APPOINT, AND PAY FOR, SOMEONE TO DO THIS FOR YOU AS YOUR AGENT?

- HOW LONG DO YOU INTEND TO KEEP THE ASSET FOR? IS IT A MEDIUM-TERM OR LONG-TERM INVESTMENT?

- HAVE YOU FACTORED IN ALL THE ASSOCIATED COSTS OF THE PROPERTY YOU ARE ABOUT TO INVEST IN, SO YOU CAN CALCULATE YOUR TRUE NET RETURNS AFTER COVERING THOSE COSTS?

WHAT IS YOUR EXIT STRATEGY - HOW AND WHEN WILL YOU SELL YOUR BUY TO LET PROPERTY, IF THAT IS WHAT YOU INTEND TO DO?

3. BUYING TO RESELL WITH PROFIT

While investment in rent-generating properties offers a very safe, consistent and passive income, you can aim for a more substantial one-time profit at the time of reselling properties you purchased or developed previously at a lower cost.

Whatever the purpose is of your investment – be it to generate rental income or otherwise – all properties you invest in are subject to the possibility of appreciating in value. The difference here is that when you buy properties with a direct aim to resell at a higher value, you often disregard every other possible benefit the property could generate in exchange for making a significantly higher one-time profit on resale.

Here are some questions to consider when you are targeting capital gain:

WHAT IS YOUR BUDGET?

MORTGAGE OR CASH: WHAT IS YOUR FUNDING METHOD?

ARE YOU BUYING LAND TO DEVELOP AND BUILD FROM SCRATCH, OR BUYING OFF-PLAN, UNDER CONSTRUCTION OR READY PROPERTIES?

WHICH REAL ESTATE SEGMENT ARE YOU LOOKING AT: RESIDENTIAL, COMMERCIAL, LUXURY OR AFFORDABLE?

WHAT IS YOUR TARGETED INVESTMENT TERM?

WHO IS YOUR TARGET AUDIENCE AT THE TIME OF RESALE? WHO IS GOING TO BUY FROM YOU AND WHY?

- **WHILE HOLDING THE PROPERTY OWNERSHIP, WHAT ARE THE DYNAMICS AND MARKET FUNDAMENTALS IN THE SEGMENT AND/OR THE GEOGRAPHIC LOCATION?**

- **WHAT PHASE OF THE MARKET CYCLE ARE YOU ENTERING? DO YOU EXPECT TO EXIT (RESELL) DURING THE SAME CYCLE? OR WILL THE MARKET BE SUBJECTED TO A DIFFERENT CYCLE AT THE TIME OF EXITING (RESELLING)?**

I have expanded a lot more on capital gain in Chapter 7.

4. CORPORATE INVESTMENT

You might be looking to buy property to run your business from, rather than paying rent, and/or investing in real estate properties or land as an extra revenue stream to run alongside or support your core business. Investors like this often use the profits from their core business to purchase real estate as a stable regular income source, or as a speculative investment for short or long term growth. Almost all large successful corporations have a certain level of exposure to real estate investment.

Questions for you – and your business partners, if you have them – to ask yourselves:

- **WHY IS THE BUSINESS BUYING AND NOT RENTING? WHAT ARE THE BENEFITS, AND WHY HAVE YOU CHOSEN THIS POLICY?**

- **IS IT IN LINE WITH YOUR FIVE YEARS BUSINESS PLAN FOR YOUR COMPANY? HOW DOES INVESTING IN PROPERTY FIT IN WITH YOUR OVERALL VISION?**

- **WHAT IF YOU HAD TO CHANGE YOUR BUSINESS PLANS? CAN YOU EASILY RENT IT OUT TO A DIFFERENT TENANT?**

WHAT IS YOUR BUDGET? WHAT CAN YOU COMFORTABLY AFFORD WITHIN YOUR PROJECTED CASH FLOW, CAPITAL GROWTH, EXPANSION ETC?

CASH OR MORTGAGE? WHICH IS THE BEST OPTION FOR YOU - PAYING IN FULL IN ONE LUMP SUM OR SPREADING THE COST OVER A NUMBER OF YEARS?

WILL THIS UNLOCK NEW VALUE FOR YOUR BUSINESS?

WHAT IS YOUR EXIT STRATEGY? HOW AND WHEN WILL YOU SELL THE PROPERTY, IF THAT IS WHAT YOU INTEND TO DO?

5. PROFESSIONAL INVESTMENT

The final group of investors we are looking at are those thinking of real estate investment as a full or part time career, either working for themselves, as part of an investment group...or as an employee of a large investment institution, advising and doing business for them.

If you are a professional investor I am sure you have already created a successful business model and are following it, so you will already have gone through the process I've outlined for the other four investor categories.

I hope, though, that this book will enhance your knowledge and provide you with some food for thought - for instance, about the way you use data, optimise opportunities and react to market cycles. One of the things which inspires and motivates me is a constant hunger for new insights and knowledge which can benefit my business, and I am sure you are the same.

If you are considering taking up a career as a professional investor, or are already in the business but looking for a new or more suitable organisation to work for, I would like to share my experience and offer you some guidance on the next page.

An important question for everyone: *It is of course possible to be in more than one of these groups, but whichever one or ones you are in, the same principles of sound investment apply – and I'll be going into those in Sections Three and Four of this book.*

First of all, though, there is a simple but absolutely fundamental question you need to ask yourself:

WHEN IS IT TOO EARLY OR EVEN WRONG FOR YOU TO INVEST IN REAL ESTATE?

Can everyone invest in real estate? Absolutely YES, but NOT if any of the following situations applies to you:

- You are overly exposed or cannot afford to be financially exposed to new investments.
- You don't understand the market.
- You don't want to invest the time to identify the right knowledge partner, consultant or agent.
- You cannot invest the required time and effort to understand the market yourself.

In brief, if you can't afford the investment and any associated risk then you should think twice before proceeding. I would not recommend it. But even more crucially – and this is one of the most important messages I can communicate to you – if you are unable or unwilling to put the time and effort into understanding the market and gaining the knowledge you need to make sound and informed investment decisions, either yourself or through a trusted advisor, you are not ready to become a successful investor.

If you are confident that you are ready for investing, it's time to move on to the next stage, starting off by making the right first steps... so let's go! I am delighted to be your guide as we look at how to ensure success for you and your investments.

INTERESTED IN A CAREER IN REAL ESTATE INVESTMENT?

Before we leave this chapter, I have a message for anyone who has been inspired by my personal story in Section One and who might be interested in joining the real estate industry as an agent to start a career in the business. If, when you have read it, you feel that it could be right for you, feel free to contact us at fäm Properties as we are always looking for self-motivated individuals to join us, and we would be happy to talk to you. In the Conclusion section of this book, I leave you with some valuable insights related to taking up real estate as a long-term profitable and professional career.

SECTION THREE

YOUR JOURNEY BEGINS

An investment in knowledge pays the best interest

— BENJAMIN FRANKLIN

CHAPTER 6

SETTING OFF ON THE RIGHT FOOT

KEY POINTS:

- TEN ESSENTIAL STEPS
  - ONE – KNOW YOUR MARKET
  - TWO – INVEST IN A KNOWN NEIGHBOURHOOD
  - THREE – ASSESS AND SELECT YOUR EXPERT SUPPORT
  - FOUR – COMMUNICATE AND COMPARE
  - FIVE – EXIT STRATEGY
  - SIX – ASK QUESTIONS AND ALWAYS VISIT THE SITE
  - SEVEN – CONSULT YOUR EXPERTS
  - EIGHT – NEGOTIATE WISELY AND DON'T HESITATE
  - NINE – CONCLUDE THE TRANSACTION
  - TEN – ESTABLISH A LONG-TERM RELATIONSHIP WITH YOUR EXPERTS
- THE MARKET CYCLES MATTER
  - IN BOOMING MARKETS
  - WHEN THE MARKET IS DOWN
- READY FOR THE NEXT STEP ON YOUR INVESTMENT JOURNEY?

WHETHER YOU ALREADY have a little experience in real estate investment, or are completely new to the market, by the time you have reached this point in the book you will understand that it's not about luck and speculation. It is about following a well-tested process that leads to succeeding in one of the most rewarding and safe types of investment ever known. There is no doubt that it is one of the best ways to create and to enhance your wealth.

TEN ESSENTIAL STEPS

Setting off on the right foot is absolutely crucial to real estate investment. But how do you do it? Here is my guide to the steps you need to take in order to hit the ground running on your journey towards achieving real success with your investments.

ONE - KNOW YOUR MARKET

After having established your investment criteria, budget, objectives and preferences by following the guidance in Chapter 5, you need to gain a general understanding of the market. Visiting different areas, developers, brokers, websites, portals and maybe developments too will provide you with a foundation for this understanding.

TWO - INVEST IN A KNOWN NEIGHBOURHOOD

It is always beneficial to start your first investment venture in a neighbourhood that you live in, have lived in or know well from visiting often. This will help you to accurately carry out all the other steps that lead to a successful investment. But obviously, if you happen to spot a much better area or project elsewhere, you should go for it. The process will be the same, the only difference being that you will have to invest more time and effort to find out all the things you need to know.

THREE - ASSESS AND SELECT YOUR EXPERT SUPPORT

This is a massively important step, not only when finding the "knowledge partner" I have mentioned before, but also any and all other expert professional support you might need – for instance, for tax, legal and property management functions. First of all, examine and assess their general approach to conducting real estate business. For this you need to:

1. **Qualify** the way they present different investment opportunities.

2. **Assess** what kind of commercial case they are presenting for their investment advice, and how they support its viability.

3. **Check and validate** the data and market statistics each expert has offered to build your investment case on. We expand on this in Section Four, Chapter 9.

4. **Establish** how long the real estate expert has spent in his or her current company. Are they short-term thinkers or long-term thinkers? If they worked short-term with their previous employers, then they could be short-term with their clients too. Look at their market or area and their project-related experience, response time, their background in meeting their promises, overall customer experience and, absolutely crucially - their value system.

5. **Discern if they publish regular market reports** on data and trends? Do they have a proven **track record** of sales or leasing? What can you read from their website? How many years have they been in the business? Do they understand the local market well? Or are they just an international brand with little or no local experience?

6. **Assess their technological prowess:** An expert or knowledge partner with prowess in technology enables you to leverage their technological tools and platform to serve your best interests. It is imperative that you understand how their technology will help you to make smarter

decisions - a tech-savvy company can give you a huge competitive advantage over other investors who still deal with old school brokers who don't use modern technology when identifying and seizing market opportunities.

7. Factor the company and the brand, not just the individual: No matter how experienced one individual is, he/she can only cover so many services. It is therefore important to look closely at the brand and the company that they work for, to identify how many of your post acquisition needs they can cover. Do this now, because it is not efficient to have to go through the same lengthy but important process of identifying the most trustworthy service provider for those future needs.

For example: if you are buying off-plan property under construction, does the expert's company provide licensed property handover services and engineered property snagging and inspection services so they can assist you at the time of taking handover of your property? Does it offer leasing and property management services to help you find, screen and qualify suitable tenants? Does it offer resale services, to help you on the resale when you want to exit? If you want to resell, does this particular real estate consultant also specialise in resale? More importantly, does it only offer these services using third parties? Or are they a licenced service provider – and best available for these services or not? It's important to establish all these things as most brokers will tell you, "buy and we will do everything for you later on". You need to know how true that is.

FOUR - COMMUNICATE AND COMPARE

Once you have identified the right property expert, clearly convey your investment target, investment terms, and preferences to them. Then compare the pros and cons of the different offers they present to you. In Section Four, Chapter 10 of this book, I will show you a practical method you can apply to compare the different offers and conclude which one or ones provide you with the best value for your money.

FIVE - EXIT STRATEGY

It is important to consider your exit strategy from day one, based on your targeted investment term. Ideally, as I mentioned earlier, real estate investment is always a medium to long term. Ask, learn, analyse and understand who is going to rent or buy from you. Based on today's fundamentals and facts, what will demand be like for your real estate around the time you have targeted for your exit?

SIX - ASK QUESTIONS AND ALWAYS VISIT THE SITE

Make sure that you leave no stone unturned or any grey areas of uncertainty. The right real estate expert should be able to clarify all your questions, concerns and doubts ... but it is also essential that you visit the site you are thinking of investing in. Don't ever make an investment based on just seeing a sales and marketing pitch, a mock-up or even a video. Always go and view the property and any neighbouring projects.

SEVEN - CONSULT YOUR EXPERTS

1. Tax: There are no set rules for the best tax structure as it can completely differ from market to market and it is highly influenced by the type of properties as well as your investment term and your equity vs bank money ratio - not to mention the fact that it keeps changing and evolving.

My advice here is to only seek tax advice from a tax-expert – not from your agent, developer or even from your lawyer. As you have to plan the best possible tax structure before buying – not after – always connect with a tax expert and consult them on the best structure prior to investing. So, if I take the Dubai real estate market as an example; Dubai is considered a tax-haven for real estate investors as, on all residential properties, there is no capital gain tax, inheritance tax or tax on rental income as of January 2022, but there is a tax on commercial properties. If you are buying a hotel apartment property (unit) it is subject to tax as it is considered as commercial and not residential, hence it is subject to tax.

2. Legal: In most cases, it is advisable to seek legal advice from a specialist real estate lawyer on any binding contract you are about to sign, to ensure that all mutually agreed commercial terms are applicable and protected under your contract. On the same note, it is worth mentioning that lawyers are usually not the best commercial advisors. Get every party to stick to doing what they do best. Lawyers are not there to advise you on the commercial elements of an agreement.

EIGHT - NEGOTIATE WISELY AND DON'T HESITATE

It is not always about pushing the other party to lower the price. You would be surprised to know how sometimes milking the seller for the last penny can actually harm your investment. So, don't be greedy and don't delay your decision – the whole point of following a very well tested and systemised qualifying process is to ensure that you are making the right decision. Don't overthink it – be confident and make your move. I'll tell you more about this in Chapter 11, which is all about negotiation and closing the deal.

NINE - CONCLUDE THE TRANSACTION

When you have done all this it's time to get on with actioning your plans. Make sure you keep all your documents, floor plans, location maps, snagging reports, ownership documents, payment receipts etc. well organised and stored safely.

TEN - ESTABLISH A LONG-TERM RELATIONSHIP WITH YOUR EXPERTS

You have invested time, money, and effort in identifying them, so make the most of that valuable relationship.

Property experts will always call the most reliable investor first when they identify great investment opportunities.

THE MARKET CYCLES MATTER

Once you become a real estate investor, you will be playing the role of either buyer or seller, depending on the market and your intentions. You are now in the game for big bucks and naturally, you want your investment to work for you and make you richer.

However, there are some ground rules you need to be aware of, because the market works differently in boom times and down times.

IN BOOMING MARKETS

- Landlords are very hesitant to sell as they aim for higher prices. Naturally, because they are hoping to get the best price they can for their property.
- Owners of prime assets ask for colossally high prices. With the market thriving, they believe they can cash in at the top.
- Prime properties become very expensive and hard to acquire. If you're looking at buying in the heart of town or in a posh locality, prices will be hitting the roof.
- Demand is higher than supply. Buyers and tenants hope to buy or rent suitable properties - but they know that landlords have the upper hand.
- Hence, what drives the decision of most buyers and tenants is really their budgets and what properties they can secure according to their financial means.

WHEN THE MARKET IS DOWN

- Properties become fairly affordable because the tables have turned, and supply is greater than demand.
- Most landlords are motivated to sell or to rent out their properties.
- Prime properties become more accessible and affordable – making it the ideal time to buy.

- Since it is now a buyer's market, buyers and tenants become very selective. They know that they have the upper hand and are determined to get the best property they can on the market.
- Hence, what drives the decision of most buyers now is how attractive the property is and how prime its location is.

Understanding the state of the market is very important for you, whether you are a buyer or a seller.

For example: if you invest in an average property in a given project, you have to factor that exiting from this property (selling/cashing out) during down markets will always be challenging. If you want to have a property that you can sell easily at any time despite the market cycle, you may have to consider investing only in the most prime properties in any project. So, if a project offers different layout, sizes, views and/or quality of materials, choose the best of everything because as I said, the best will always sell despite market conditions.

We will talk more about market behaviour in various stages of the 'boom and down' cycle in Chapter 8.

READY FOR THE NEXT STEP ON YOUR INVESTMENT JOURNEY?

Before we move on, I'd like you to ask yourself the following questions to track your progress and ensure that you're on the right path.

- WHY do you want to invest in real estate?
  - To create passive income.
  - To live in.
  - To preserve your wealth.
  - To profit from capital appreciation.
  - To run your business from.
- WHERE do you want to invest? Do you know the area?
- What is your BUDGET?
- HOW will you finance the investment? Are you going to use bank money? If yes, how much?
- What are your medium or long-term OBJECTIVES? In other words, do you have an exit strategy?

When you have asked yourself those questions and answered them, map out your investment journey and the time, money and effort resources you may require. Ensure that you have a timeline to reach each milestone and start out your journey.

CHAPTER 7

HOW DO REAL ESTATE INVESTORS MAKE MONEY OUT OF THEIR INVESTMENTS?

KEY POINTS:

- CAPITAL GAIN
- RENTAL INCOME
  - **CALCULATING YOUR ANNUAL NET RENTAL INCOME**
  - **SIX KEY FACTORS TO CONSIDER**
  - **PROFESSIONAL SUPPORT, AN ESSENTIAL TOOL**
  - **SOLE OWNERSHIP**
  - **CO-INVESTMENT**
    - Real Estate Crowdfunding
    - Real Estate Private Equity
- FACTORS WHEN BUYING OR INVESTING FOR RENT GENERATION
- FACTORS WHEN BUYING OR INVESTING FOR CAPITAL GAIN
- THE BIG DECISION
  - **CREATING WEALTH FROM REAL ESTATE INVESTMENT: RENTAL INCOME OR CAPITAL GAIN?**

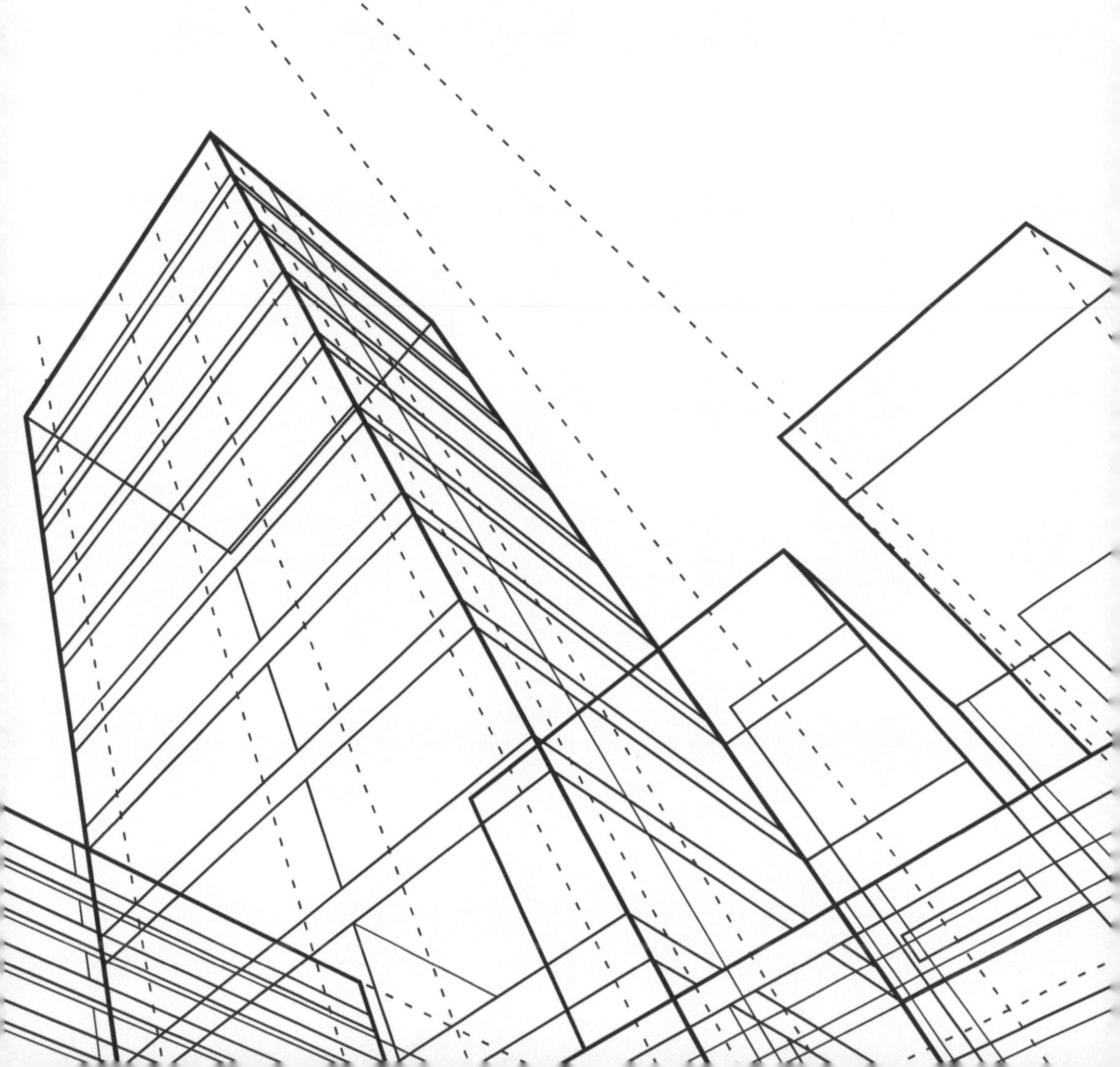

THERE ARE TWO ways in which real estate investors make money on their investment: through rental income on their property, and by appreciation in its value, i.e. capital gain. In this chapter we will be looking at them both in depth. We will be going into some detail, so please read this detail carefully as it all adds up to help you make the best – and most profitable – investment decisions.

CAPITAL GAIN

'Capital gain' is when you buy a property or any kind of real estate asset at X and sell it at X + profit.

In order for you to achieve profit you have to sell at a higher price than you bought at of course, and in order for you to sell at a higher price you have to have purchased under-priced property which you can then sell at market price. Or bought a well-priced property and held it for a period of time until the property has increased in value – which can happen for various reasons, as explained here.

Alternatively, you might buy older and slightly run-down or mismanaged properties, refurbish them and set up the right management system so you can sell them at a higher price. Or construct or develop a property to sell at market price.

All that sounds simple, but it is also important to understand that the natural appreciation of real estate value (or indeed any form of investment) comes as a result of either:

1. **Macro triggers:** Growth in the macro (large scale) market – when the overall economy and in particular real estate does well in a given market. As a result of that, every single project in that market witnesses price appreciation.

2. **Micro triggers:** Increase in asset value for one or more specific real estate segments whereas other real estate segments or locations are experiencing a different, steady or even sometimes a downtrend. A good basic example would be the impact of e-commerce on the retail shop segment that has started to suffer as people buy online. Conversely, the warehousing segment has started to witness a high demand from all the giant e-commerce companies like Amazon and others. As a result of such micro fundamentals relevant to that specific segment, there would be an appreciation in capital, despite the macro market staying as is. For instance, imagine that you bought a property in an underdeveloped area and two years later a metro station, shopping mall and large park were created there – that would be enough micro fundamentals to push the price of properties up, irrespective of the general state of the macro market of the city, where values remain the same. This is also a good example of how your experienced knowledge partner can have market-intel that would enable you to identify potential real estate investment opportunities that are under the radar.

What's interesting here is the fact that the underlying story behind the increase in value of your property going up is often rental prices. As I explain later, in Chapter 10, for those who are buying income-generating properties the correlation between rent generated and price is very strong. For instance, if the average annual rental return in the area is 5 per cent and the rent is 50,000 then my sales price is 1 million, and if the rent went up to 100,000, the selling price of the property would reach 2 million as 100,000 is 5 per cent of 2 million.

Coming back to what I have previously mentioned about hiring a professional property manager, you can now clearly see how enhanced rental income can substantially increase the value of your assets, enabling you to profit from capital gain.

In the same way, taking out mortgages (using borrowed money) to invest in rent-generating properties can increase your returns on equity, and using bank loans to invest in properties while targeting capital gain can also substantially enhance your returns. For instance: if you bought a property for 500,000 using 400,000 (80 per cent) of the bank's money and 100,000 of your own capital (20 per cent) and you manage to resell the same property over time for 750,000, your ROE is 250 per cent because your profit is 250,000 and your invested capital is only 100,000.

But remember, higher returns often come with higher risks, and I strongly advise you to read carefully what I write in the next chapter about the best and worst times to use bank money to invest in real estate, so you can make fully informed decisions.

RENTAL INCOME

This is the most basic form of gaining secure and easily accessible income based on real estate.

How much can you generate per year?

Typically, across the world, you can generate anything between 3–5 per cent as gross rental income per annum when you invest in prime locations. In sub-prime locations, you can expect to generate more or less anything between 6–10 per cent gross rental income per annum. This also depends significantly on what sort of property you are investing in – a large asset (a full building or one apartment), commercial or residential and others.

It is important to note that these 3–10 per cent annual rental income figures is calculated based on the total value of your asset.

For instance, if your property is worth 1 million and your annual rent is worth 50,000, your gross rental income is 5 per cent.

Some of you might be wondering how many real estate companies – including, but not limited to, brokers and developers – can promote offers with much higher rental returns than 3–10 per cent per year.

Sometimes this is a marketing ploy which simply ignores or hides many underlying costs and unpleasant hidden factors.

In these cases, the "net returns" are based on Return on Equity (ROE), not on Return on Investment (ROI).

Put simply, this means it ignores any money you may have borrowed from the bank or the property seller or developer in order to make your investment. It only takes into account your own direct investment and thus substantially (and deceptively) enhances the percentage of your annual returns.

So, if you buy the property mentioned in this example for 1 million and pay 250,000 as a down payment – with the other 750,000 being bank money – your annual rental income of 50,000 works out as 20 per cent of your invested equity, and that is your ROE. Whereas the same 50,000 of rental income works out to be only 5 per cent ROI.

In other words, the ROE is calculated based on your invested capital, whereas the ROI should be calculated based on the total value of the investment, which is in this case the total value of the property.

Often the ROE percentage is labelled as ROI in marketing spiels and sales pitches because it shows more attractive numbers, hypothetically speaking.

If – in the example we are using – they asked you to invest 100,000 in a property worth 1 million, based on the fact that 900,000 is borrowed from banks and the property is rented for 50,000 per year, the ROE is 50 per cent whereas the ROI is 5 per cent. That is why you see such cases advertised as 50 per cent annual ROI.

With these factors in mind, investors should never blindly follow the advertised percentage of returns but also dig deeper to understand how it has been calculated.

CALCULATING YOUR ANNUAL NET RENTAL INCOME

There are several elements you need to take into consideration when calculating what your net rental income per annum will be:

1. **Expenses** You need to deduct all your yearly expenses out of the total: the remaining amount is your net rental income. In practical terms, this means factoring in the costs that may come with renting the property out to tenants. Typically, you have your annual property service charges, maintenance work, utilities (depending on the contract with your tenant), taxation, real estate agent fee, property management fees and so on.

2. **Occupancy** An additional element which many real estate investors fail to factor in is occupancy. If you have a property that should generate 50,000 per year, you should always allow for the fact that it might take a few days, weeks or maybe longer to rent it out, depending on the market situation.

3. **Fluctuation** You should also factor in market price fluctuation, which can push your property rental income up or down. The good news, though, is that it will never drop to zero, which is why property is such a safe investment.

Please note that annual rental income, when calculated as a percentage of the total property price, is often referred to as Gross ROI and Net ROI. You should now understand the difference between gross and net in this context.

THERE ARE TWO WAYS IN WHICH REAL ESTATE INVESTORS MAKE MONEY ON THEIR INVESTMENT – RENTAL INCOME AND CAPITAL GAIN.

SIX KEY FACTORS TO CONSIDER

There are six key factors that you should consider when investing in income-generating properties. Depending on your budget, your commitment levels in terms of time and effort, geographic location, asset type and others, there are several ways of 'getting into' investment in commercial or residential properties to generate rental income and we'll be looking into those shortly. First of all, though, I'd like to remind you of some of the key factors you need to keep in mind.

1. Total acquisition cost
2. Occupancy level
3. Rental value
4. Ongoing associated costs (maintenance, service charges etc)
5. Legal framework
6. Tax implications

PROFESSIONAL SUPPORT, AN ESSENTIAL TOOL

Before we go any further, a word about ensuring that you have the right support in place – as we have covered earlier when talking about knowledge partners and other specialist professionals.

You will never hear me advising you to get a professional real estate agent to create the right legal framework or tax structure for you, because that's not what real estate agents do best. Similarly, management of your property cannot be fully optimised unless you engage a professional property management manager – not a real estate agent or even yourself (unless you happen to be a property management professional).

Depending on the type of property there is a wide spectrum of critical aspects which have to be managed by a property management expert. These range from screening and qualifying tenants to collecting rent on time, following up any due or overdue payments, running preventative and ongoing maintenance, looking after tenant retention, optimising all costs associated to the property such as utilities, cleaning and security, coordinating with your lawyer, rent increase, technical support and so much more. As you can see, it's a lot of detailed work and that's why you need a property management professional.

Now, with these considerations in place, let's look at those different ways of investing in property to let:

SOLE OWNERSHIP

You can simply buy an apartment, villa, office or any other type of property as the sole owner and lease it out on a short- or long-term rental basis.

In order to do this efficiently you either need to spend quality time and effort on managing your property, the tenancy contract and the tenant – or hire a professional property manager to do that on your behalf, as I have suggested.

Please note in Section Two, Chapter 3, I provided examples of what you should avoid when investing in, or buying, rent-generating properties – especially if you are offered a guaranteed annual rent. Very often this kind of 'guaranteed' investment comes with unpleasant hidden costs and catches.

CO-INVESTMENT

Although I always prefer to have full control over properties I own, certain situations and circumstances can lead us sometimes to partner up with others in one way or another.

You can acquire income generating real estate as a co-investor by participating in an investment pool with partners you know – or through real estate crowdfunding, real estate private equity firms, REIT real estate investment trusts or other similar structures.

The ideal way of co-investing – whether it's through crowdfunding, private equity or a real estate trust – is with a partner supported by a team of professional real estate experts. Those experts can qualify opportunities according to 'best practice' procedures and also manage the assets or properties in the most efficient and productive way, in order to generate the highest income possible.

Most firms with this support in place, especially the reputable ones, also have the capacity and experience to obtain leverage from banks (mortgages), which can play a major part in enhancing your return on equity.

REAL ESTATE CROWDFUNDING

Typically, real estate crowdfunding enables investors with modest budgets to enter the real estate market by investing small amounts, which can start from as little as 1,000 dollars, in order to co-own a rent-generating property. If you are investing as a fractional owner in a small to mid-size asset, you are – in most cases if not all – paying a decent premium as compared to directly acquiring the full asset under your name, which is fair as it costs money to create and manage the entire set up behind it. A better way to is to invest, probably the same amount, but in a much larger asset (mega assets that are difficult to be acquired by individual investors) as you are more likely to benefit from the discounted "bulk rate" the crowdfunding platform is achieving due to the size of the transaction.

REAL ESTATE PRIVATE EQUITY

With Real Estate Private Equity, you are one of a pool of private and/or public investors who buy, finance or own property as a group.

That means you are not in sole control of the investment – and, as I have previously indicated, I have never been a fan of that, as in most cases you are obliged to hand a wide range of management rights over to asset managers. In some circumstances, though, it can be the ideal investment vehicle for any specific needs, preferences or targets some investors have.

If you decide that investing through private equity is for you, these are five 'red flags' you should look out for:

1. Ownership structure and investing under a fiduciary agreement: The most critical aspect is the legal ownership structure.

- Investors must ensure that they directly own shares in the asset or in the SPV (Special Purpose Vehicle) that directly owns the asset.
- No layers of ownership can be present in between because it can expose them to a high risk.
- Investors should also avoid any fiduciary based investment agreements where their ownership rights are governed under a secondary agreement between them and the real estate private equity company, or one of its subsidiaries.

What is most dangerous is when investors own shares in a shell company, which owns another SPV (Special Purpose Vehicle) which, in turn, owns the actual asset. This means, if any legal issues arise in the shell company over financial problems on other projects, you may end up with drastic compromises affecting the interests of the project you have invested in – along with endless other potentially damaging scenarios.

So, when investing through private equity, you should always ensure that you own shares in the company which directly holds the deeds of the asset you are investing in.

2. Investing in an over-priced asset: Always study and review the valuation report and ensure that it is provided by a reputable evaluation firm, before focusing on any guaranteed rental yields.

3. Not having a defined exit strategy: When considering investment via the private equity route, it is essential that you factor in the term of your investment and have a predefined approximate exit plan.

4. "Too good to be true" returns, exposing you to risk which outweighs the benefit: Real Estate Private Equity firms often offer fixed rental income over a set period of time, backed up by a rental contract with a reputable tenant. But some assets come with a guaranteed rental structure engineered to offer great yields, with the rental value set higher than it should be, which could be due to:

- The rental contract was signed a few years ago when prices were higher. Investors should always check the rental index for the location of the project and see if current rents are in line with the rental agreement. Why? Because when the current rental contract ends, the property will be leased on the actual rental value – which in this case would be lower than with the previous rental contract, and that can drastically impact the value of the asset.
- A much worse scenario could be when the rental contract has been engineered in agreement with the tenant – or when the tenant is the actual seller. They sign a higher rental agreement, so the price – often based on a certain number of multiples of the rent – will be a lot higher than what it is actually worth, and the extra rent will be recovered in the extra profit they make as a result of selling for a much higher price. In these circumstances, when the fund manager looks for a new tenant towards the end of the agreement, at current market rental prices, the value of the asset will drastically drop.

  For example: An asset is evaluated at 70 million (7 million x 10 years) based on an inflated 10-year rental contract of 7 million per year, offering investors 10% annual rental yield – whereas the actual rental market price is only 5 million per year. At the end of the ten years, for the asset to be sold and still offer 10%, the new selling price will be only 50 million (5 million x 10 years), so there is a drop in value of 20 million.

There has to be a healthy balance between the rental income, the loan-to-value on the actual asset, the total purchase price of the asset and the property evaluation report.

5. Lack of clarity on rental yields: Always ensure clarity about whether the rental returns are based on unleveraged (i.e. without a loan or debt) or leveraged (with a loan or debt) investment in properties and that, either way, those returns are within a healthy range.

- When you are offered a 5 per cent rental yield on a 10 million asset, without leveraging the asset, it means that your rental income is 500,000.
- If you are offered the same 500,000 but as 10 per cent rental yield on a leveraged asset worth 10 million, the asset has a loan-to-value of 50 per cent. 5 million has been invested by you and the other 5 million comes from a bank loan – hence your 500,000 rental income forms 10 per cent of your invested capital.

So, when you are offered a real estate investment opportunity that generates x per cent rental returns per year, always investigate whether it is based on a mortgage or not. The difference is that with leverage comes risk. If the market should for whatever reason drop by 50 per cent, it means you lose all your money – because the other 50 per cent of the asset's value will go to the bank to cover the loan.

In following chapters I will explain in detail the risks and the opportunities involved in using bank money to invest in real estate, because it is heavily impacted by the market cycle.

FACTORS WHEN BUYING OR INVESTING FOR RENT GENERATION

1. Property acquisition costs: Not just the actual price of the property but also any other associated costs. You often see people calculating their rental income 'off the cuff', without factoring in their full acquisition costs. For instance: they think that a property offered at 1 million which rents for 50,000 provides a 5 per cent rental income. However, the accurate calculation is in fact 1 million + stamp duty + tax (if applicable) + acquisition costs, which all add up to the actual total cost. Only when you know the full total costs can you accurately estimate the gross and net rental income.

2. Ongoing costs: Always be clear about future annual service charges and regular maintenance and property management costs, so you are able to calculate your net rental income after deducting all expenses.

3. Property management: It is important to have a clear understanding on how you are going to manage your property. Are you going to do it yourself? Or are you going to use a professional property manager?

4. Occupancy levels: When you calculate your rental income, make sure you factor your occupancy level. If the anticipated annual rent is 50,000 per year, you should allow for a couple of weeks as a transitional period between one tenant and another. Of course, this also depends on the type and nature of the property.

5. Long- vs short-term rent: Do your sums, explore both options and see which one is more profitable. This will depend largely on the location and the type of property. Contemplate which option is more financially rewarding, after calculating all associated costs to both kinds of rental modules – short and long term. In fact, each module has its pros and cons, hence it is important to factor the immediate direct financial benefits, as well as the long-term benefits, and how they align with your long-term plans and exit strategies. For example, in a long-term lease, landlords are obligated to keep tenants for a medium to a long period of time, whereas, in short-term rental modules, landlords have more liberty to vacate their properties and maybe sell to end users who are normally prepared to pay higher than savvy investors buying rented properties. Another basic example: in short-term rental modules, landlords can increase their prices every time there is a new tenant (if the demand supports it); this cannot be the case with long-term modules.

So it is not only about which one generates more money today, it is about weighing the financial benefits in the light of your medium- and long-term investment objectives.

6. Existing and new rental agreements: If you purchase a property which has a sitting tenant, it is already generating rental income – but you should always benchmark the value of the rental contract against current market rental prices. Why? Because if you bought a property rented out on a contract signed three years back at a higher rent than today's market, you will have to factor in that on renewal the current tenant – or a new tenant – will be looking for a rent which matches the current market levels. Similarly, it is okay to buy a property that is not generating high returns as rental income, if the rental contract is about to expire and the new contract will be at a higher rate (you might also consider carrying out some improvements on the property to boost the rental income even more).

7. Ownership period and future property value: How long do you want to keep the property for? What is your exit strategy? Who are your tenants during the ownership period – and who are your targeted buyers at exit? Yes, it is true that you can never figure this out 100 per cent at the time you are acquiring a property, but it is important to form a basic understanding of these considerations.

8. Location, prime or sub-prime: The quality of location is reflected in higher or lower rental returns – so never turn a blind eye to the future value of the property you are looking to buy for rental returns. True, you may be getting higher ROI and ROE on rent when you buy in sub-prime locations, but the future value of the property can be impacted by low construction quality. Standards in sub-prime locations are normally lower than in prime locations, whereas prime locations are often not only of higher quality but also more limited in supply and hence offer better future value. Think about this scenario: you have the budget to invest in prime rental properties, but you go for sub-prime because it offers 8 per cent annual income as compared to 4 per cent from a prime property, but – and it is a big but – the sub-prime property might appreciate by 10 per cent over five years and the prime property 100 per cent over the same time span. I give you this extreme example to explain the principle: there is no clearly defined rule to follow, as there are too many other variable factors such as your budget – but I thought it was important to provide you with some food for thought.

9. Taxation: Always get tax advice from a tax expert, not from your real estate agent. Remember to take capital gain tax into consideration as well as tax on income generated as applicable in your market.

10. Fully paid off or mortgaged: How do you intend to fund your property investment? Are you going to use bank money or only your own? I would strongly recommend that you pay close attention to what I have to say about the best and the worst time of taking up a mortgage in Chapter 8.

FACTORS WHEN BUYING OR INVESTING FOR CAPITAL GAIN

1. Triggers for capital gain: As I have already explained, increases in property value can be due to different factors. If you are targeting capital appreciation you have to be clear on the fundamentals which will push the value of your property up – and your target audience for selling the property on exit.

2. Funding strategy and cash flow: How are you going to fund your investment? Using bank money, a payment plan from the real estate developer you are buying from – or are you going to fully fund it yourself? What are the anticipated gross and net ROI and ROE for each scenario?

3. Risk analysis: Always evaluate the risk of market change. What will be your best position when markets go up and what will it be if the market goes down?

4. Off-plan (under construction) or completed property: Each has its own pros and cons, but both can be very profitable.

5. Taxation: As with investment for rental income, always get tax advice from a tax expert and not from your real estate agent when investing for capital gain.

6. Term of investment and cost of money: You could be investing in an off-plan property targeting capital appreciation when sold on completion or at any other point of time, always factor the opportunity cost of your invested capital. If you make 20 per cent capital gain after holding for four years, that is 5 per cent per year (annualised capital gain) and if you make the same capital gain of 20 per cent within six months, your annualised capital gain is 40 per cent because you made 20 per cent in just six months.

7. Exit strategy: Always factor in the "how" and "when" of your exit strategy.

THE BIG DECISION

CREATING WEALTH FROM REAL ESTATE INVESTMENT: RENTAL INCOME OR CAPITAL GAIN?

Is there a clear demarcation between the two, or is one better than the other?

As you will have seen from the examples discussed for both rental income and capital gain, each can be a very lucrative and safe investment when done correctly. While rental income secures a reliable and steady return on investment, capital gain is also amazing – because you often get a large lump sum of money all at once when you cash out on your investment.

However, I want to give you the safest recommendation and the one I follow myself. *That is: always factor both streams – rental income and capital gain, because they work closely together.*

If, for instance, you want to sell but the market is not offering you a profitable opportunity to exit, you shouldn't leave it empty but put it up for rent – so at least you can generate some rental income until better exit opportunities come along. On the other hand, if you're buying a property purely with the purpose of generating steady rental income, it is still always sellable – and remember, the healthier the net rental income the higher the price, and the capital gain profit you will make on selling it.

In other words, when you are buying a property aiming to achieve *capital gains*, always look closely at the possible rental income, because it's an important indication of the future value of your property – and it could be a source of steady income until your exit.

And if you are investing in real estate targeting only *rental income*, always remember that acquiring a well-priced property can substantially enhance your rental returns – as well as increase the value of the property, should you decide to sell it one day or even refinance it to release some equity.

Now that we've arrived at the conclusion of this chapter I'd like to end with this simple message: It's all about the buy.

If you buy a property at the right price-point and you factor all the impactful numbers, you will always be able to achieve a healthy rental income as well as being able to cash it out with good capital gain profits.

It's a win-win!

A SOUND INVESTMENT REQUIRES TIME, MONEY AND EFFORT. MAKING AN INVESTMENT IS A MAJOR RESPONSIBILITY, AND YOU HAVE TO LIVE UP TO IT.

CHAPTER 8

UNDERSTANDING REAL ESTATE INVESTMENT MARKET CYCLES

KEY POINTS:

- THREE KEY CONSIDERATIONS
    - **DIFFERENT MARKETS REQUIRE DIFFERENT STRATEGIES**
    - **WATCH OUT FOR GET-RICH-QUICK SCAMS**
    - **WHAT YOU SHOULD KNOW ABOUT INVESTING IN BOOM AND DOWN MARKETS**
- THE GOLDEN RULE
- DOS AND DON'TS DURING DOWN MARKETS
- DOS AND DON'TS DURING BOOM MARKETS
- USING BANK MONEY TO INVEST IN REAL ESTATE DURING DIFFERENT MARKET CYCLES

AMERICAN BUSINESS magnate, investor, and philanthropist, Warren Buffet, once said, "Look at market fluctuations as your friend rather than your enemy; profit from folly rather than participate in it."

The property market, like other investment avenues, is not static. As mentioned earlier, it is cyclical with boom times and down times. If you are reading this book, you are either a part or want to be a part of the market, either as a buyer or a seller.

It is therefore essential for you to understand how real estate buyers, sellers and even tenants behave during different market cycles. By the end of this chapter, you will understand how to navigate the market and how to strategise your choice of property, your market entry and exit as well as your financial arrangements, based on each market cycle.

THREE KEY CONSIDERATIONS

DIFFERENT MARKETS REQUIRE DIFFERENT STRATEGIES

Studies have revealed that the average investor makes decisions based on emotion, more than logic – buying high on speculation and selling low when panic sets in.

It always shocks and disappoints me to see many people making serious investment decisions during certain market phases; it's as if they are living in a directly opposite phase. Because of this, they end up missing the genuine opportunities presented by the market cycle current at that time.

Your entry, term of investment and exit strategy are always heavily impacted by the market cycle you are in. So, the first step is to understand the cycle you are in and to strategise accordingly. As an investor, you can never change the mainstream direction of the market. You have to learn how to profit by travelling in that same direction. Real estate is a medium- to long-term investment, and if a profitable short-term exit presents itself, then why not!

WATCH OUT FOR GET-RICH-QUICK SCAMS

Those investors who look for shortcuts and get-rich-quick schemes more often than not fall victim to scams and con artists. Why? Because, as any rational and sensible person understands, there are no shortcuts. They know that scammers across all industries make pie-in-the-sky promises that are too good to be true. And aren't.

WHAT YOU SHOULD KNOW ABOUT INVESTING IN BOOM AND DOWN MARKETS

Every cycle imposes different investment rules, and smart investors learn to master both.

In his article, 'Why Real Estate Cycles Matter', Matthew Montagu-Pollock says, "Real estate markets tend to fluctuate between undervaluation and overvaluation. What is 'high' for a market, and what is 'low' is largely a matter of history, and of comparison with other assets. Overvalued property markets are extremely seductive. There are often good reasons to believe that a particular market deserves higher valuations than it did in the past, or than other markets deserve. And sometimes (to make matters more complicated) these arguments are right."

THE GOLDEN RULE

In order to maximise profit and minimise risk, you have to align your entry strategy, your term of investment and your exit strategy with the market cycle you are in.

As a general rule, as an investor, you need to recognise that it's actually safer to invest during down markets than boom markets. That does not mean that you cannot profit from a booming market. But it does mean that you have to be more careful and very clear about your financial holding power, investment term and exit strategy.

As a savvy real estate investor in a boom market, it is highly recommended that you have a medium-term plan wherever possible if you are buying – because any long-term plan may not be in line with the natural course of market cycles. Which means that all of a sudden you find the hard-earned capital you're investing is subject to completely different market conditions as a booming market is bound to calm down or become steady at one point of time or another.

Nevertheless, if you have solid financial holding power, so you are not under pressure to fire sell, you can play the long game with the investment term and exit at the best point in the market cycle. Whatever comes down is also bound to go up again, and the general graph of any real estate market over a long period of time is always up.

However, during down markets, your plan will always work at some point sooner or later. That means good timing and understanding of the real estate cycle is vital to truly maximise your return on investment.

*****

Now we're going to delve deeper into how each market cycle offers different types of opportunities depending on your investment appetite, and how each cycle requires a different mindset and strategy. I'll also talk you through what you need to do during either cycle to be successful.

DOS AND DON'TS DURING DOWN MARKETS

DO...

✓ **Acknowledge the prevailing negative mood of the market and its benefits for you.** If you ask people about investing in real estate in a depressed market, nine out of ten will respond with panicky and negative answers. You need to be wiser and understand why it's exactly the right time to invest.

✓ **Remember that although the market is down, better times are bound to come.** You don't have to wait for the very worst point of the down market – the only way you'll know that the market has bottomed out and is starting to bounce back, is when it actually has started to. By then, you'll have missed a given opportunity. Why? Because at that point, whoever you are buying from will also have identified the same trend and put their prices up.

Find the right knowledge partner. As I have mentioned at length in previous chapters, real estate experts can enable you to access a world of opportunities and make great profits in a down market. ✓

Use bank money during down markets. This can maximise your ROI like never before; I'll show you how later in this chapter. ✓

Identify, acknowledge and accept the main triggers behind the falling market. Markets can go down for many different reasons – it is important to understand which of those reasons apply, so you can plan your next steps accordingly. ✓

Estimate the duration of the current market challenges. You can't precisely predict the future, but it is always good to establish a possible time frame for when those current challenges will come to an end, or change. ✓

Look for opportunities created by setbacks to the market during the down phase. Target prime locations, prime projects and prime units within the areas that interest you. This is exactly what will immensely maximise your profit at exit: buying the best at the greatest value prices. ✓

Identify the risk factors but don't let them hold you back. This is unless you believe that you cannot afford the risk. Know your boundaries and your comfort zone. Then make the move and invest. ✓

DON'T...

Overthink the opportunity to buy and do nothing while "waiting for the right moment". Get moving, don't stop searching for a good opportunity and when you ✗

find it, don't hesitate. Follow the steps mentioned in this book and you cannot go wrong.

X **Overthink your exit strategy if you're selling, either.** Work with whatever fundamentals and facts you currently have in hand; it takes a crystal ball to accurately predict the future and we are not in that business. Your knowledge partner should be able to sit with you and work out exit strategy guidelines covering who is going to buy from you, why and when.

X **Panic over short-term market turbulence.** The market may still fluctuate. Hold your ground and don't get anxious. It will come back up.

X **Lose touch with your knowledge partner.** After making the transaction, keep in touch with them every now and then. You never know when a golden exit opportunity for your investment might come their way.

X **Be greedy.** When the right exit opportunity appears, exit at that time. And exit quickly if you encounter any outstanding or unrealistic rise in prices, because any sudden rise is bound to go down again.

DOS AND DON'TS DURING BOOM MARKETS

DO...

✓ **Be sensible and ensure that you are not taken in by over-positive hype.** Just because maybe nine – if not ten – out of ten of the people you speak to might have something positive to say about investing during a flourishing market, it doesn't make them right. Far from it!

✓ **Ensure that you hold your nerve** and take a completely rational business approach.

✓ **Find the right knowledge partner.** That is a given in either scenario, or I cannot stress this enough.

Ensure it is actually a boom market and not a bubble market. For this you need to: ✓

- Compare current price trends to the historical price trends.
- Identify the fundamentals behind the price boom.
- Understand how long property prices have been going up for.
- Forecast how long the fundamentals that pushed the market prices up will last for.
- Cooperate with your knowledge partner to understand the price differences between constructing a property from scratch and buying a ready-built property.
- Look at whether banks are lending more or less to mortgage buyers. After the 2008/9 mortgage bubble crisis, banks became far more conservative when it came to property loans. So, it follows that when banks are providing buyers with higher LTV (loan-to-value), it is often an indication of a healthy market. It means the banks have faith in the value of the property market they are funding/financing.

Develop your exit plan from day one. Look for opportunities that offer a clear exit plan, in line with your investment end goals. ✓

Define your short- to medium-term exit strategy: ✓

- Who is your target audience for resale?
- Why would they buy from you?
- Who will you be competing with during your exit period?
- Build some assumptions around a timeframe to exit.

Identify the risk factors but don't let them hold you back, unless you believe that you cannot afford the risk. Know your boundaries and your comfort zone. Then make the move and invest. ✓

Watch the market closely with your knowledge partner. ✓

DON'T...

✗ **Be greedy.** Stick to your exit strategy and be flexible. When you are investing during market booms, remember that sooner or later price will either start falling or it will stabilise. No one can identify the exact price peak of any market: as long as you are making a decent profit, don't look to max it out – make your exit, if that is what you planned for at the time of entering the market.

*****

Now that you've learnt about market behaviours and you understand what to do during a boom market and a down market, let's learn more about the correlation between using bank's money to invest in real estate and the market cycle you are in:

USING BANK MONEY TO INVEST IN REAL ESTATE DURING DIFFERENT MARKET CYCLES

Using bank money to invest in the real estate market enables investors to truly maximise the returns on the equity they have invested. It is not the best strategy, however, across all market cycles.

While using bank money is one of the best strategies to invest in real estate during challenging or down markets, it is, on the other hand, the riskiest strategy to follow during booming markets when prices are sky-high.

Here's how it works... Let me explain this to you in numbers through this simple case study, illustrated on the next page. Please note that this is a hypothetical example that does not factor different costs nor potential earnings. Please just focus on the most basic numbers in order to grasp the principles.

As you can see, using bank money in a booming market exposes you to a risk you may not be able to afford. In this example, you invested 250,000 dollars and took a loan from a bank for 750,000 dollars. The market went down by 50 per cent so the market price for you to resell or to exit from your investment is just 500,000 dollars. However, because you owe the bank 750,000 dollars, you have to pay out another 250,000 dollars from your own pocket in order for you to resell your property. Which is a risk that you may not be able to afford.

In conclusion, if you exited at 50 per cent of your original purchase price, you would lose your down payment of 250,000 and you will have to inject another 250,000 to pay the bank back, in order for you to sell out the property and be free of debt.

On the flip side, if you use bank money to purchase a property in a market that's down, you will be able to achieve the sort of high returns you would never achieve without bank money, even if you use your full equity to invest. Far, far more than you are ever likely to achieve by saving part of your salary every month. In other words, it can be your starting point for building up serious wealth.

In this example, you bought the property at 500,000. You paid 125,000 from your pocket and you added 375,000 from the bank. Your risk is very limited because you are buying a property at half price as compared to its price during booming markets.

You have the opportunity to double and triple the cash/capital you invested.

What do we see from this example? You need to be very careful when you use bank money to invest during booming markets, and you have to be very clear on your investment plan, factoring all the important elements we spoke about earlier in this book. On the flip side, you cannot possibly get a better opportunity to leverage on bank money to invest in real estate than during down markets.

Managing the risk... Of course, every investment comes with a degree of risk. There is no such thing as

	Booming Market	Down Market
Property value	1,000,000	500,000
Loan value	750,000 (75% of the purchase value)	375,000
Invested equity	250,000 (25% of the purchase value)	125,000
	Assuming that every booming market has to come down at some point of time. The market went down by 50% over a number of years.	Assuming that every down market has to come up at some point of time. The market went up by 50% over a number of years.
Resale value	500,000	750,000
Profit or Loss in numbers	**-500,000**	**250,000**
Returns on invested equity	**-200%**	**100%**

FIG. 1: An example showing the risks of using bank money for investment in booming vs down markets.

a completely safe haven in the real estate market. For instance, look at the London market and how it reacted to "Brexit", or the Hong Kong market and how it reacted in 2019 to the political uprising against mainland China.

But real estate remains the most secured and, in most cases, the least affected market when compared to capital and equity markets, where your investment can go to zero.

If you follow the steps discussed in this chapter, and you have factored in and assessed your risk factor well, you will certainly be able to mitigate those risks to the best possible extent. Even if you don't win big, I assure you that your risk will remain minimal, while your upwards potential is sky-high.

Keep calm and carry on... Remember, the markets are cyclical so there will be times when there's a rise, and times when there's a fall. Don't panic and don't give into greed. Letting your emotions drive your investments is a sure-fire way to disaster – don't get too carried away when the market is booming or too disappointed when the property market nosedives.

Always keep calm and consult your knowledge partner, who is an expert on the subject. As Benjamin Franklin famously said, "An investment in knowledge pays the best interest."

In Section Four, I will explain how you can identify the right property to invest in through a sequence of well-defined and easy to follow steps.

SECTION FOUR

DESTINATION: SUCCESS

Believe you can and you're halfway there.

— *THEODORE ROOSEVELT*

CHAPTER 9

THE ABSOLUTE IMPORTANCE OF DATA, PRICE TRENDS AND MARKET STATISTICS

KEY POINTS:

- DATA: THE NEW OIL
- MINIMISE RISK, MAXIMISE POTENTIAL
- SUCCESS DOESN'T COME BY CHANCE
- WITHOUT DATA, YOU ARE RELYING ON OPINION AND GUESSWORK
- HOW TO ACCESS, READ AND UTILISE DATA
    - **STEP ONE: GATHERING DATA**
    - **STEP TWO: TRANSACTION HISTORY AND TRENDS**
    - **STEP THREE: EVALUATING THE OFFER**
- READING AND INTERPRETING THE DATA
- A SIMPLE GUIDE TO THE PROPERTY EVALUATION PROCESS
    - **RENTAL INCOME**
    - **COST OF LAND AND CONSTRUCTION**
    - **COMPARATIVE MARKET ANALYSIS (CMA)**

NOWADAYS, THE BUSINESS world operates around two major pillars: data and technology. However, many people still make some of the biggest and most serious investment decisions in their life without looking at the data and statistics which is at their fingertips. They turn a blind eye to it, failing to utilise a comprehensive range of easy to use and helpful technology which can add enormous value to their decision-making process.

To make the most accurate forecasts, you require a lot of data and statistics.

ASK YOURSELF THIS QUESTION: HOW CAN YOU SEE AND IDENTIFY FUTURE OPPORTUNITIES BEFORE OTHERS?

As an investor, you are – in one way or another – competing with other investors for the best real estate opportunities. You cannot win against investors who use data and statistics to drive their investment strategies from entry to exit unless you are equally, if not better, equipped.

So, it is important to understand that investment is not only about buying or selling properties, but also about making the right data-based decision at every important stage: entering the market, reselling, renting or exiting your real estate investment.

Data allows you to gain insights and make sound forecasts about future trends that will enable you to make the right investment decision, minimising your risk and maximising your potential for profit.

Here's some good news: it's much easier than it may seem.

Many people are intimidated by the idea of having to read data and look at charts. But in reality, it is very simple, and you don't need to be an expert to achieve the required results. By the time you are done with reading this chapter, you will:

- Understand the importance of data when it comes to real estate investment.
- Understand the major kinds of data and trends to look for.
- Learn how to read it and utilise it.

Please note that although all the charts and images used in this chapter as an example of how data and statistics work are taken from the Dubai real estate market, the same framework of data and market trends is applicable and accessible in most, if not all, mature markets.

DATA: THE NEW OIL

Once upon a time, those who controlled oil, controlled the economy and had the power. Today, data is the new oil.

Making any investment decision without looking at the relevant numbers, data, and statistics is the equivalent of making one of the most important and serious choices in your life, while blindfolded.

The 2020 Covid-19 pandemic reminded us that no investment is without risk. No one ever thought that airplanes would one day stop flying, that airports would close down, roads would be empty, and people would have to stay at home. With these severe market changes, once-in-a-lifetime opportunities were born across most markets. Investors who managed to remain objective and read through the historical and current data and market trends managed to make the most out of those opportunities and create new wealth. Situations like that are beyond our control when they happen, but navigating through them and managing our next move *is* within our control.

MINIMISE RISK, MAXIMISE POTENTIAL

What we *can* do is minimise risk should any sudden global crisis arise, while maximising profit potential while everything goes as forecasted.

There is no other way to do this other than backing up every decision throughout our investment journey with facts, data, and statistics. I guarantee you that most people who end up losing money on their investments haven't studied the data, statistics and market trends well enough prior to making their investment decisions.

SUCCESS DOESN'T COME BY CHANCE

Real estate is one of the most rewarding investments on earth. Almost every single rich individual has a decent part of his or her wealth invested in real estate assets. In fact, many successful entrepreneurs today, and in the past, have made more money in real estate than what they made in their core business. But people don't get rich by chance; it takes time and energy to plan and execute a successful strategy. Get that right and there is nothing more rewarding, as I have already emphasised in earlier chapters.

But you won't get it right if you don't do your homework. And what makes that homework easy is the data and information you have at your fingertips, 24/7.

As a buyer or as a seller, it is not so much a *wish*, but a *need* to know the exact and true value of properties and projects you are interested in. The same applies to landlords who own income-generating real estate assets, in order for them to calculate their actual rental income based on today's market price evaluation.

Even for real estate sellers, it is essential to understand the true value of their real estate assets so they can set the right selling prices. The price you see in the adverts is not necessarily the true value of the transaction, as often sellers advertise at a higher price than what they will actually accept, to leave some space for negotiation. Also, some online ads may show very attractive prices in order to attract prospects and obtain their contact details, whereas in reality the true price of the advertised property is higher than advertised.

In conclusion, the most reliable source for the true value of real estate is the price based on actual sales transactions which take place, as registered in the government land/real estate department records.

WITHOUT DATA, YOU ARE RELYING ON OPINION AND GUESSWORK

One of the most distinguishing features of any mature real estate marketplace is the transparency of data and statistics, which you rarely see in new marketplaces.

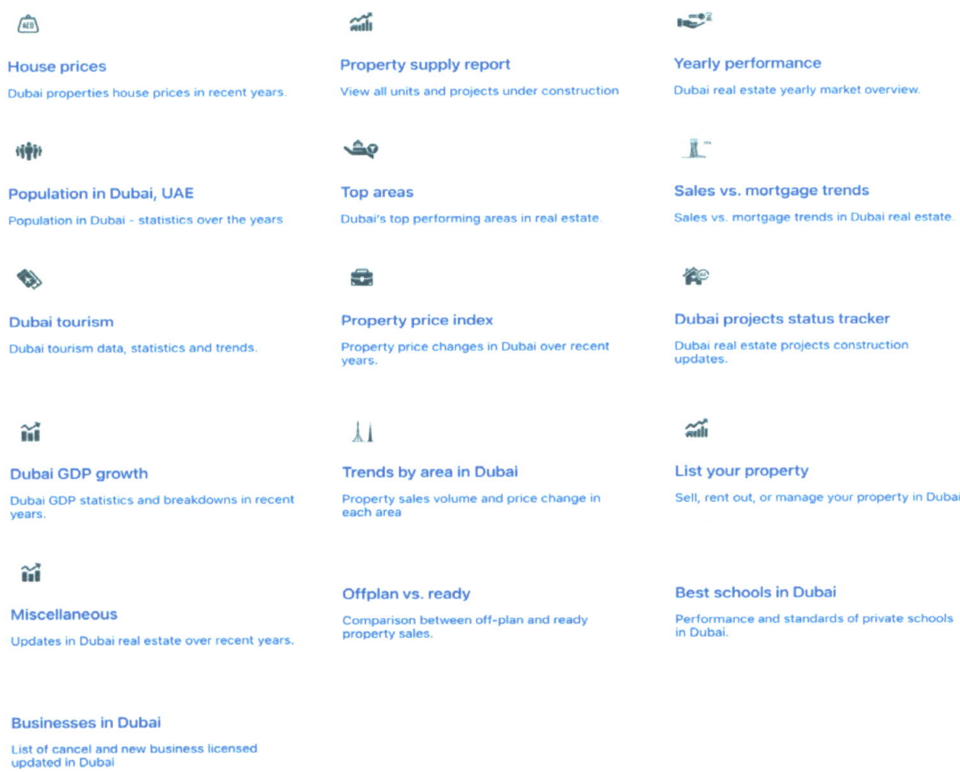

FIG. 2: An example of the kind of reports you can get about the real estate market in Dubai. Sourced from www.DXBinteract.ae.

Whether you want to buy or sell real estate property, you need to first fully understand the true value of the property, so you can maximise your profit. You might ask for an expert opinion, access online property portals and check the advertising prices of similar properties – or seek a paid property evaluation provided by a third-party independent property evaluator. But the most accurate value indicator is the historical data along with the most recent transaction prices, as found in the Government Registry free of charge here in Dubai, and in similar sources in most mature markets around the world, based on national data. Some are free, some may require payment of a subscription or other form of fee.

That's how you will find the true value and trading history of the property you are buying or selling – by accessing its actual trading data.

HOW TO ACCESS, READ AND UTILISE DATA

I'm now going to take you through this essential process in three easy steps, followed by a brief guide on to how to read data and the property evaluation process.

STEP ONE	STEP TWO	STEP THREE
Gathering Data	Transaction History and Trends	Evaluating the Offer

Here are some helpful definitions for the four levels of scale used in this three-step process:

- **Level 1 – Overall market,** the one right across the city in which you are investing. It also has to be segment or type specific; for example, if you are investing in apartments, then you have to see the overall market in the city in which you are investing for apartments.
- **Level 2 – Master community,** the area where the project is located. It also has to be segment or type specific. For example, if you are investing in a certain master community that consists of apartment, villas, offices and retail shops, make sure that you do your research and gather data that is specific to the type of real estate in which you are investing within that master community.
- **Level 3 – Project,** the real estate development of which the property is an integral part (for example, a complex, building, tower, villa, community, etc).
- **Level 4 – Property,** the specific real estate unit in which you are interested.

STEP ONE: GATHERING DATA

There are four essential data trends, which are:

1. Median price per square foot
2. Total number of sales transactions
3. Total value of sales transactions
4. Current and future property supply

The first step is to gather data for the four trends at each of the four levels of scale mentioned above and according to the specific timeframe you choose (for instance, it could be three months, six months, three years or ten years) as well as the specific type of real estate in which you are investing (whether the property or project is ready or if it is off-plan, i.e. newly built and sold directly by the real estate developer).

FIG. 3: Chart showing the stages of gathering data for the four trends at each of the four levels of scale.

1. Establish a median price per square foot at every level, that is, the sale price in the middle of the data set when you arrange all the prices from low to high. (Please note that if there are unreasonable extreme numbers or data at either end of the set these should be ignored.) Then ask yourself or your knowledge partner:

- Why did the median price appreciate or depreciate over a certain period of time? Is it because of the overall state or mood of the economy, or micro-triggers (e.g. local market conditions or trends) related to the project?
- Am I buying at the peak of the price trend, at the middle or at the bottom?

2. Establish the total number of sales transactions at all four levels, and ask yourself or your knowledge partner:

- How many properties of the same type were sold in the past month or year(s)?
- How many properties in the same project or master community or market were sold? How did the number of transactions trend up and down?

The answers will tell you how fast landlords in this project can exit. Also, when you see this data in the light of your rough estimate of the number of properties offered for sale on the market, you will be able to conclude whether there are (a) many sellers but no buyers, or (b) many buyers but no sellers – and thus understand the level of demand and supply.

A low number of transactions with a healthy price trend can be an indication of having many buyers and few sellers (high demand and low supply) which is very healthy. But if you see a downtrend in the number of sales transactions combined with depreciating prices, it is an indication of low demand and probably higher supply.

3. Establish the total value of sales transactions at each of the four levels, and ask yourself or your knowledge partner:

- What is the total value of sales transactions registered for the similar properties within the same project or master community?
- Has the total value of sold units within the same project or master community or market been increasing or decreasing over the past years? Why?

- Has the total value of sales transactions been trending up or down in the past few years? Why?

This indication is used more at the scale of the entire market or the master community, but it can also form indications at the project or the property level. It helps you understand whether lower or high value projects are being added to the community or market, and to see any sharp increase or decrease in property prices. Or, in some cases, it can tell you if there are any upgraded, fully furnished or refurbished units that caused any sharp uptrend.

4. Understand the current and future property supply at all four levels, an essential step that is beneficial to answer the following questions related to the supply and demand factor:

- Are there new projects under construction, to be built or completed in the same master community or market over the coming few months or years?
- How many more units will or may come to the market and when?
- Will new projects be more attractive or offer better prices or more facilities?
- How would the new supply impact the current and future demand on the property and the project I am buying in?

Like other assets, real estate depends on the law of supply and demand. When demand for property is high, but availability is scarce, prices go up and it becomes a *seller's* market. And, when the number of available properties increases and the market is glutted, prices typically drop, and it becomes a *buyer's* market.

Supply and demand in real estate are not easy to balance. If the demand goes up suddenly, property prices skyrocket. Understanding this basic economic principle can help consumers decide when is the best time to buy or sell their properties.

The supply of properties should be studied, based on the available stock in each area and the lifestyles offered by that supply.

You therefore need to ask how many ready-to-sell projects and how many under-construction projects are located in the area in which you are buying. It is essential to understand the current as well as the future supply of projects in your micro and macro market, especially when factoring your exit strategy – which will often depend on having long-term demand from buyers and tenants.

The charts in the following pages illustrate the market trends mentioned here. Please note that these sample charts are from the Dubai market and are purely to illustrate what you should be looking to find out and establish for your own market and projects.

I have sourced these from www.DXBinteract.com, which provides access to reports for investors in the UAE market. If you are in this market, I recommend you look at the reports on this website as it enables you to start a broad search at the city level and explore different parameters and criteria, such as location, ready projects, off-plan projects, mortgage transactions, cash transactions, apartments, offices, villas and others. Basically, it is important to estimate the overall market performance across the different segments and types, but at the end of the day, you are going to invest in one specific location or project that is either ready or off-plan, apartment or a villa or others. Hence specifying your search and narrowing it down to the specific category of real estate is vital to developing and obtaining the right insight. The times of reading broad reports are over; it is the era of interactive reports that enables you to narrow your data-gathering process to exactly what you need.

Once you are done with step one, you will have established a clear understanding of the price cycle, the supply and the demand of the overall market, the master community, the project and the property you are analysing. You are now more than half-way through understanding whether you are buying or selling at the right price and time. In step two, you will go into the details at a unit level.

DON'T BE INTIMIDATED OR DEMOTIVATED BY THE "DON'T DOS", BECAUSE KNOWING WHAT YOU SHOULD AND SHOULDN'T DO WHEN INVESTING WILL MAKE THAT INVESTMENT BULLETPROOF.

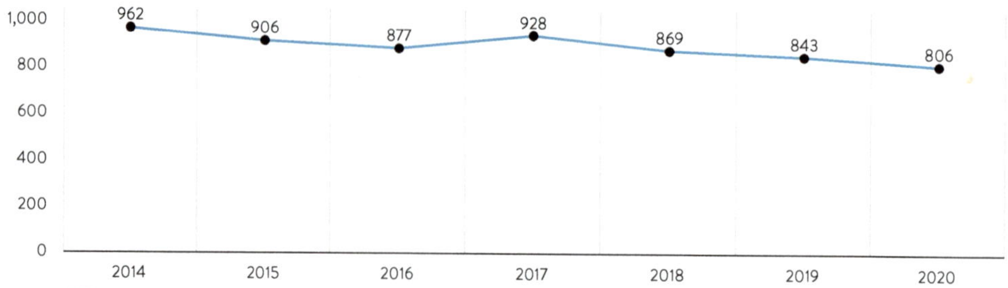

FIG. 4: Chart showing the median price per square feet trending over a given period of time. (Source: www.DXBinteract.com)

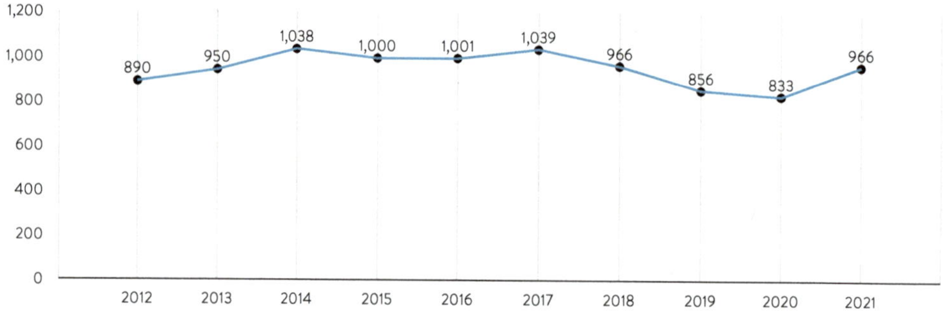

FIG. 4A: Chart showing the median price per square feet trending over a period of time for the overall market (Source: www.DXBinteract.com)

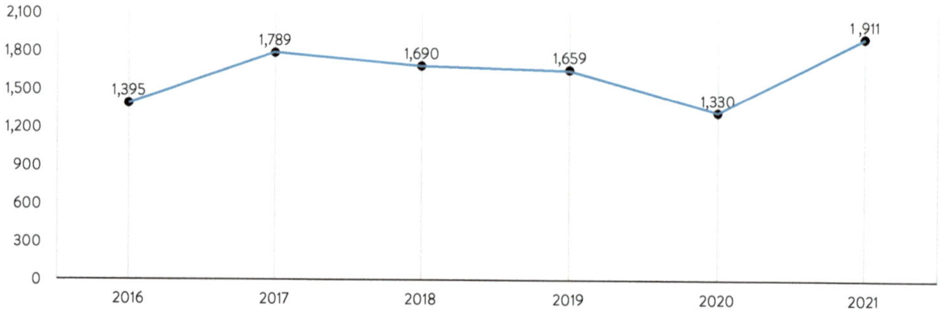

FIG. 4B: Chart showing the median price per square feet trending over a period of time for a specific master community. (Source: www.DXBinteract.com)

AREA	TYPE	VOLUME 2019	VOLUME 2020	VOLUME CHANGE %
Abu Hail	Plot	8	7	▼ -12.5
Al Aweer First	Plot	137	131	▼ -4.4
Al Aweer Second	Building	-	1	-
Al Aweer Second	Plot	2	4	▲ 100
Al Bada	Building	3	5	▲ 66.7
Al Bada	Plot	8	8	0
Al Baraha	Building	2	2	0
Al Baraha	Commercial	1	1	0
Al Baraha	Plot	2	1	▼ -50
Al Barsha First	Apartment	1	4	▲ 300
Al Barsha First	Building	8	6	▼ -25
Al Barsha First	Plot	8	4	▼ -50
Al Barsha Second	Building	4	1	▼ -75
Al Barsha Second	Commercial	9	5	▼ -44.4
Al Barsha Second	Plot	9	10	▲ 11.1

FIG. 5: Table showing the price change per square feet trending in different areas of Dubai. (Source: www.DXBinteract.com)

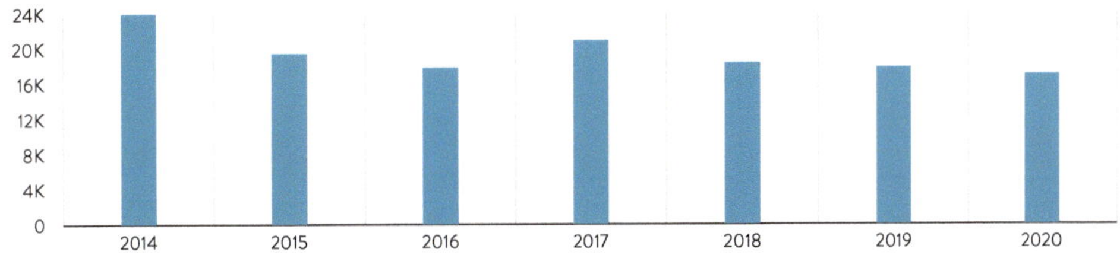

FIG. 6: Chart showing the yearly sales volume over a given period of time.
(Source: www.DXBinteract.com)

YEARLY SALES VALUE OF ALL AREAS

The property sales value in Dubai over years based on the Dubai Land Department

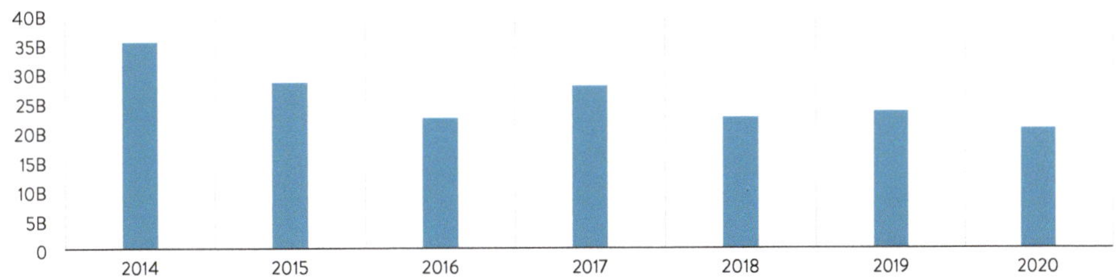

FIG. 7: Chart showing the total value of yearly sales transactions over a given period of time.
(Source: www.DXBinteract.com)

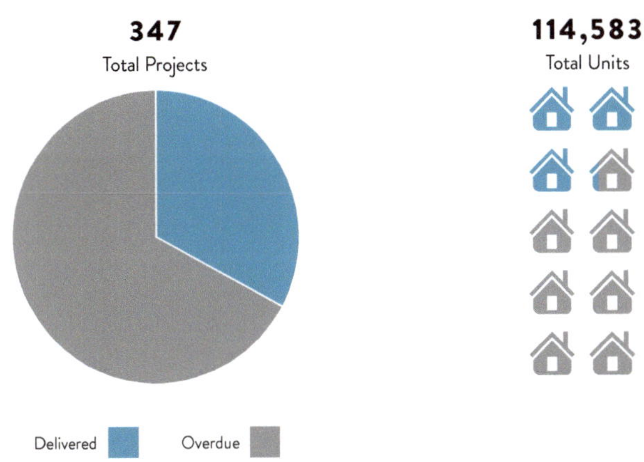

FIG. 8: Property supply report, showing the delivery rate and number of projects in 2020.
(Source: www.DXBinteract.com)

NUMBER OF YERLY DELIVERED UNITS

This chart shows number of units based on the actual completion date

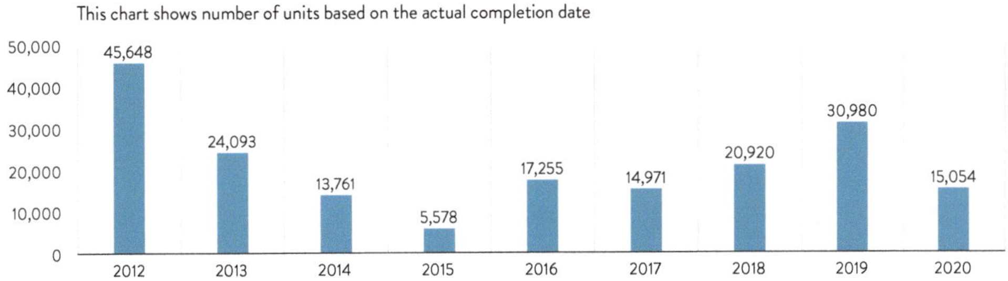

FIG. 9: Property supply report, showing the number of yearly delivered units.
(Source: www.DXBinteract.com)

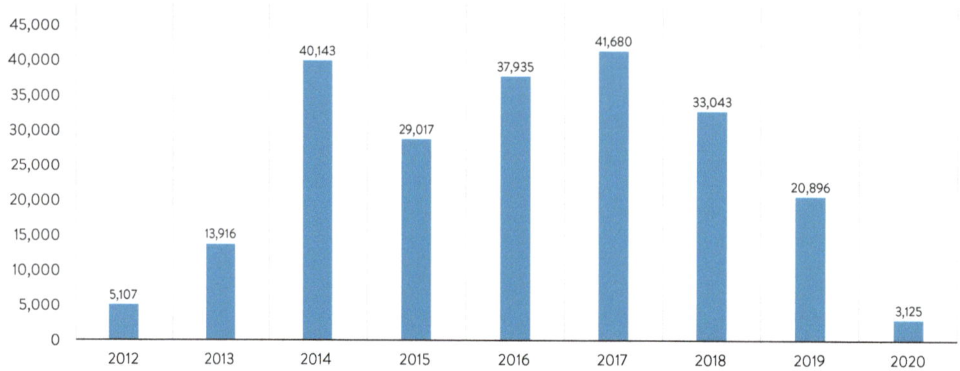

FIG. 10: Property supply report, showing the number of yearly launched properties. (Source: www.DXBinteract.com)

These numbers do not include any overdue projects with handover date prior to 2020

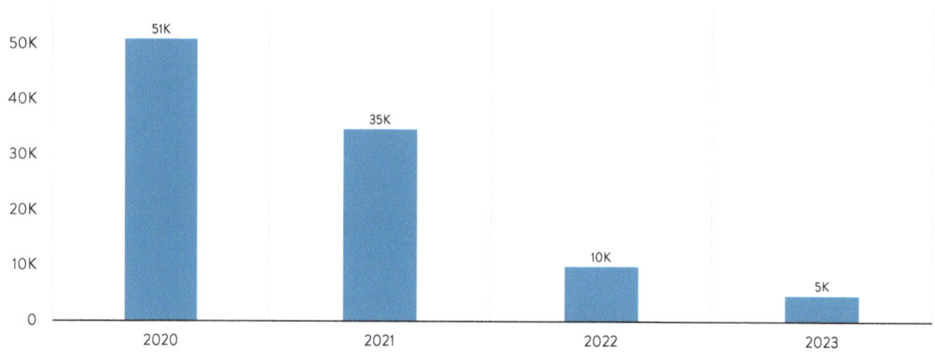

FIG. 11: Property supply report, showing the future planned property supply (as of January 2020). (Source: www.DXBinteract.com)

This chart considers properties that are under construction

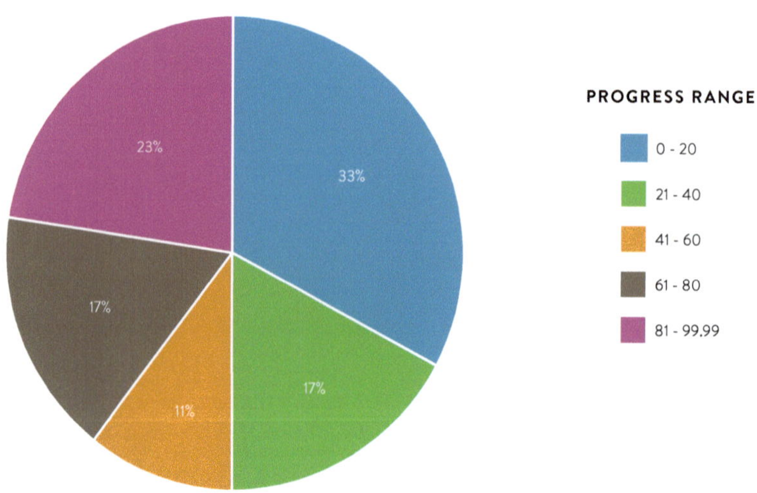

FIG. 12: Property supply report, showing the progress of construction of projects. (Source: www.DXBinteract.com)

STEP TWO: TRANSACTION HISTORY AND TRENDS

The next step is to study the price per square foot and the total unit or property value for the last five registered sales transactions for a similar property – be it an apartment, villa or land, etc.

When I say, "similar property", I mean properties which most resemble the actual property in which you are interested, in the following ways:

- Size
- Type of unit
- Furnished or unfurnished
- View
- Location
- Age of property
- Layout of property

FIG. 13: A view of the website showing the sales transaction history of a project. (Source: www.DXBinteract.com)

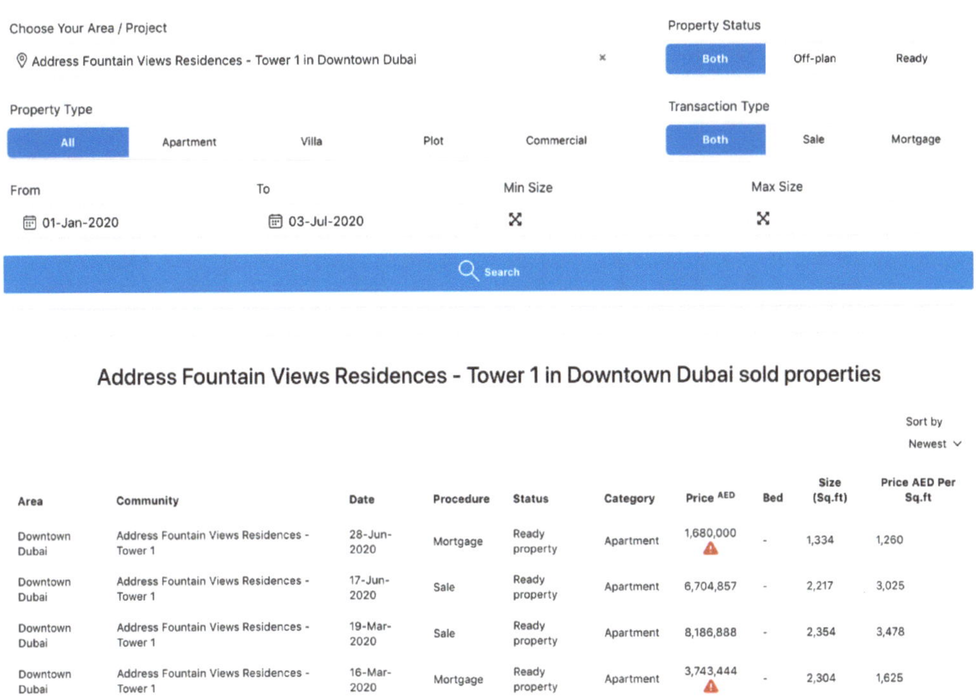

Area	Community	Date	Procedure	Status	Category	Price AED	Bed	Size (Sq.ft)	Price AED Per Sq.ft
Downtown Dubai	Address Fountain Views Residences - Tower 1	28-Jun-2020	Mortgage	Ready property	Apartment	1,680,000	-	1,334	1,260
Downtown Dubai	Address Fountain Views Residences - Tower 1	17-Jun-2020	Sale	Ready property	Apartment	6,704,857	-	2,217	3,025
Downtown Dubai	Address Fountain Views Residences - Tower 1	19-Mar-2020	Sale	Ready property	Apartment	8,186,888	-	2,354	3,478
Downtown Dubai	Address Fountain Views Residences - Tower 1	16-Mar-2020	Mortgage	Ready property	Apartment	3,743,444	-	2,304	1,625

1. Study the value of every sales transaction in your project (the price per square foot and the total price of the real estate unit). As you can see in the search box below, the project name is "Address Fountain Views Residences – Tower 1, Downtown Dubai" and you can see the table of all sales transactions registered for apartments sold in that particular tower.

So, if you have an apartment to sell in the same building – or if you want to buy an apartment – by checking this table you will be able to understand at what price value (total unit value and the value or price per square foot) similar size apartments are trading for. You can also check how many apartments have been sold within a given period of time.

2. Establish the number of sales transactions that has taken place in your project during the past three or six months. You can see the collected data related to the number of sales transactions as explained earlier in this chapter, under Step One, point number 2.

FIG. 14: Chart showing the number of sales transactions that has taken place in a project.

2,283	**3,304,308**	**15**
Median price per Sq. ft.	Property median price	Transactions
42.89% YoY	42.89% YoY	7.14% YoY

ADDRESS FOUNTAIN VIEWS RESIDENCES - TOWER 1 IN DOWNTOWN DUBAI PROPERTY PRICE OVER TIME (PER SQ. FT.)

Mortgage transactions might be registered based on the loan value; hence, this chart does not consider the mortgage transactions.

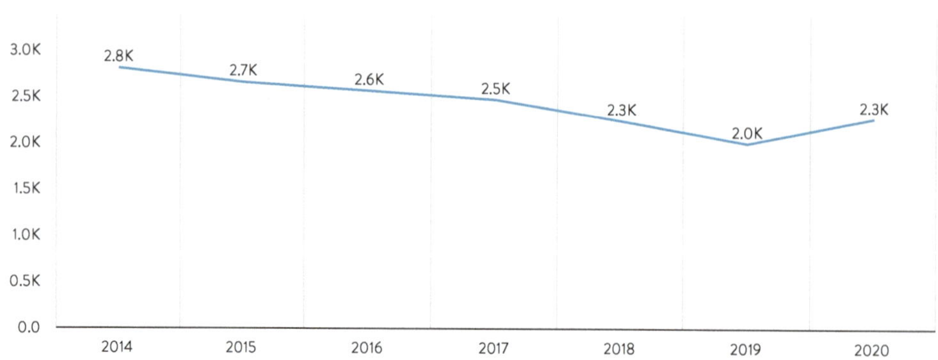

3. Payment Terms can make a considerable difference to prices. In general, there are two ways to acquire a property on extended payment terms.

- **Using a bank or mortgage provider:** In these instances, the registered property price is not impacted, as the mortgage cost is defined in a separate agreement between the buyer and the mortgage providers. The registered price per square foot and/or total property price therefore remains the same; however, there is indeed a cost impact that you can calculate.
- **Extended payment plans by real estate developers, large real estate investment institutions or similar organisations:** There is an almost infinite variety of this sort of scenario, so to keep it simple let's take "real estate developers" as the most common example. When real estate developers offer projects for sale, the offer may come with a payment plan, dependent on market conditions.

Every real estate developer ideally wants payment in full up front in a single transaction. In challenging market conditions, however, this is not achievable – so the developer has to offer an attractive payment plan to investors. These payment plans can be over a number of months or years.

In these cases, prices are impacted as the interest payable over the extended plan is always built into the price. The point I want to convey here is that it is important to analyse whether the numbers or data you are reading for the price per square foot or the total price are based on extended payment plans or not. You can check this by searching for offers and prices on the project online.

For example, let's say that a real estate developer is selling a tower of 400 apartments. Sales started in 2014 when the project was still under construction and the price per square foot was 1,000 based on a three-year payment plan. In 2017, the project was completed, and the developer still had fifty apartments to sell. However, the market was too weak for them to sell the remaining completed units. The developer therefore makes a special offer, "Move in today and pay over 8 years", but the cost of that extended payment plan increased the price to 1,300 per square foot. The extra 300 wasn't added because the project went up in value, but because of the payment plan. In fact, in such instances you may well find units in the same project bought by investors during the launch stage reselling for less than 1,300 per square foot, but without the payment plan.

As a general rule, reading data for real estate transactions and market trends is all about questioning any kind of irregular upward or downward fluctuations, whether we are talking about prices or number of transactions... then finding accurate answers to enable you to achieve an accurate market reading and hence make the right move.

STEP THREE: EVALUATING THE OFFER

Compare, analyse, qualify and evaluate the actual offer made to you – whether it is to sell or buy – with your findings covering the four levels discussed in Step One, relating to the specific property. This will enable you to understand what is:

- A fair property value.
- An overpriced property value.
- An underpriced property value.

I trust that you are now well informed about the best and smartest steps to take when buying or selling a property based on fact and hard numbers. You will also be able to judge whether you have to negotiate further before completing any deal.

These three steps represent a method which applies worldwide as it depends on prices (per square foot or per square metre, as well as total prices) and the number of transactions. You can therefore run through this process for all sorts of properties, be they residential, commercial, under construction, rented, vacant and so on.

Let me also remind you the importance of identifying the right knowledge partner who can guide you and explain to you the facts and numbers that make their offerings a valuable investment.

DO YOU NEED TO BE AN EXPERT TO READ AND UNDERSTAND DATA AND MARKET TRENDS?

The answer is NO. It is a straightforward process of reading through plain numbers, asking some basic questions and getting the answers that simply explain and guide you on the best price to buy or sell at.

As mentioned earlier, almost every mature market offers a wealth of real time and transparent data and statistics, and the basic framework of utilising data to make well-informed investment decisions applies to all markets in more or less the same way. But, since most of my wide experience is in the Dubai real estate market, I have used the Dubai model to demonstrate the process to you.

For Dubai real estate, all this data is easily accessed through www.DXBinteract.ae. All data on this website is sourced from the Dubai Land Department, Government of Dubai. You can also download the mobile application to access the same data on the "fäm Properties" website.

If you are operating in a different market, all you have to do is some research to identify the most appropriate and credible sources for equivalent data, then follow the same process.

READING AND INTERPRETING THE DATA

Accessing the data is only the first step, as it needs to be followed by thorough reading and accurate interpretation of the data. This may sound complex, but rest assured, it really isn't.

All you need to do is take some time reading the data, then start asking your knowledge partner some informed and relevant questions about why various numbers went up and down during a certain period. You will then arrive at a rational conclusion that will give you a rock-solid understanding of the market, based on indisputable numbers and facts.

A SIMPLE GUIDE TO THE PROPERTY EVALUATION PROCESS

Now we have talked about numbers, data and property value, I believe it is also worth giving you a very quick and basic outline of the property evaluation process. There are three basic building blocks for real estate evaluation, which are rental income, the cost of the land and construction, and CMA or competitive market analysis. You need to have a proper understanding of each of these to evaluate property accurately.

RENTAL INCOME

You need to build a solid understanding of the actual rent value that similar properties are already being leased for. Also find out the average expected ROI for rent in that location for similar properties. Then compare the rental value and the average rental ROI in that location against the offered property value.

For instance, an agent is advertising an apartment for 1.5 million dollars and promising investors an estimated net rental income of 5 per cent per year (5 per cent ROI). All you have to do is to check the yearly rental value of similar neighbouring apartments to assess whether the agent is over promising or if the numbers are more or less accurate.

So, if the yearly rent of similar surrounding properties is 50,000 dollars, it means that the annual ROI of the offered property is NOT 5 per cent as the agent is claiming. Assuming that the average ROI in this location is 5 per cent, it means that 1.5 million for a property that rents for only 50,000 is overpriced. Or if the 1.5 million property price and the 50,000 are the actual market rates, it means that the ROI is 3.3 per cent and not 5 per cent as the agent promised or communicated.

With this information at hand, you can conclude that to achieve 5 per cent rental income, the apartment value should only be more or less 1 million dollars. Because for the rental value of 50,000 to form 5 per cent of the total property value, the value should be 1 million.

COST OF LAND AND CONSTRUCTION

This cost is calculated by finding out the average price of the land or plot that the project or villa is built on, adding it to the average construction cost of the project, and comparing it to the offered price for the property or similar property. It is of course easier to calculate property costs for independent villas, as compared to the cost of an apartment within a skyscraper tower.

Here is a quick example: The land size is 10,000 square feet, and the built-up area (constructed internal area) is 6,000 square feet. The land price per square feet is 500 dollars and the construction price per square foot for a similar range of quality is 500 dollars. For such an example, the calculation would be:

- 10,000 (land size) X 500 (land cost per sq. ft) = 5 million (total land value)
- 6,000 (total internal constructed area) X 500 (construction value per sq. ft) = 3 million (construction cost)

Continuing the same example, let's assume that the time frame to build is two years and the total investment is 8 million dollars, with no bank loan. This means that 6 million dollars has to be invested in the first year (land cost + 1 million as partial construction cost), and 2 million dollars has to be invested in the second year (the remaining construction cost). Then the average cost of money – the amount it could earn elsewhere, equivalent to the bank rate – is 5 per cent per year. (Note: for ease of calculation, we are showing cash flow on a yearly, not monthly, basis).

- The cost of money for the first year is 300,000
- The cost of money for the second year is 400,000
- Total cost of money is 700,000

In conclusion, the total cost of a similar villa is around 8.7 million dollars. Hence if you are to buy a similar villa, anything above this price is the premium you are paying to save time and effort and to move in or to generate rental income immediately. So, if it is offered at 30 million dollars, you know it is overpriced. If it is offered at 12–13 million dollars, you are most likely to be getting fair value, depending on all the other parameters we discussed earlier. Although not every investor can run the numbers for this, especially if it is for a large complex project, it is still important for every investor to understand the basics of property evaluation that professional property evaluators use to put a price tag or value on a property.

COMPARATIVE MARKET ANALYSIS (CMA)

This is a core method used by all professional property evaluators. In essence, it is comparing similar properties to the one you are looking at, in the light of various parameters that depend on the market you are in – as well as the type of properties you are looking at. Basically, when you compare properties that are similar to the property you are evaluating the transactional prices and the listed price of property ads.

When you run a CMA, it is essential to ensure the data you are collecting is for the most similar properties to the actual property you are evaluating. To ensure that, you have to collect data for similar properties as per the following parameters, then factor in any possible minor differences when it comes to deriving the final estimated value:

- Size: total; internal; balcony/garden
- Unit type: residential, commercial, hotel or hotel apartments; number of rooms
- Furnished or unfurnished
- View: Is the unit overlooking a lake, mountain, landmark, marina, beach, park? Full unobstructed special view; partial special view; no special view – for instance, a community or street view; blocked view
- Location: middle or corner unit; direct access to beach, mall, metro station, etc.
- Age of property
- Property finishing and quality of used materials and content
- Property layout
- Offered in one full payment or on a payment plan (instalments)

Now that you have a fair idea on how property evaluation works, here is my last note on data and statistics.

*****

Having said all this, I must also say that I still sometimes hear people criticising data and statistics. Yes, manipulated data can be used as "evidence" to market and promote a lie. That is why you have to follow this simple process and factor all the core elements when finding, reading and analysing data:

1. Don't blindly follow reports. Always seek access to the open data source provided by the government, because it can never be misleading – unlike partial or selective data provided to serve a particular purpose or to paint a particular picture someone wants to achieve. Some real estate agents will pick and choose data based on the picture they aim to convey to their clients. For example, if an estate agent wants to prove to a seller that prices are low, he or she will handpick the lowest sales transactions and the lowest advertised prices and make a report based on them. But if the investor is looking at the open-source data, this becomes impossible. Similarly, if estate agents want to prove to a buyer that the high price they are offering is genuine, they will handpick the highest-priced transactions and not the average or the median price. That is way I gave the example of www.DXBinteract.com, as it gives you access to open-source data based on your personalised search criteria.

2. Don't let excel sheets, numbers and charts intimidate you. They are actually just numbers. If they seem complex, ask for assistance from the appropriate people around you.

3. Read and raise questions as you read. As you read, you may raise the same set of questions to different experts or resources and go with what convinces you the most.

In the following chapter, I am going to share with you a proven and powerful process you need to follow to make successful investments. You might find it a little technical to start with – but if you want to ensure that you're making the most accurate investment decisions to minimise your risk and maximise your profit potential, please read it all thoroughly, from start to finish.

THE RIGHT KNOWLEDGE PARTNER CAN GUIDE YOU AND EXPLAIN TO YOU THE FACTS AND NUMBERS THAT MAKE THEIR OFFERINGS A VALUABLE INVESTMENT.

CHAPTER 10

HOW COMPARISON, ANALYSIS AND ASSESSMENT CAN HELP MAKE RIGHT INVESTMENT DECISIONS

KEY POINTS:

- KEY ELEMENTS OF EVERY INVESTMENT DECISION
  - **FACTS AND UNDERSTANDING**
- THE CAAD PROCESS
- HOW TO APPLY THE CAAD PROCESS
  - **STEP ONE: COMPARISON**
    - Projects
    - Comparison Criteria
    - Information or Data
  - **STEP TWO: ANALYSIS, ASSESSMENT, DECISION**

REAL ESTATE VALUE is measured by the inch – not just the physical inch, but also every other little detail, from the view through the windows to the interior layout and the quality of the fittings.

Now that we have learnt the basics about data and statistics, I'm going to provide you with the tools to enable you to quantify those details, features and benefits, so you can establish the real value you are getting for your money, whilst factoring in the key requirements for your investment.

To evaluate and decide how great or poor a product is, compare it to two or three other products which also closely match your 'checklist' of preferences and needs – and then decide which one offers the best value for money.

In fact, comparing one product to another is an integral part of almost every daily purchase we make, whether it's real estate, cars, clothes, appliances or anything else . We all want to get the best possible value, and that's probably why we tend to consider, compare, and often ask people around us for advice – before we make our purchases.

Needless to say, real estate is a very valuable and costly investment. We therefore need to take the ordinary purchasing process to the next level and ensure that we are not missing any detail, so we can ultimately make the right decision and create, protect or enhance our wealth through our investment.

Why do we need to do this?

Brochures, marketing spiels, sales pitches, manipulated analysis, overly promising sales and persuasive marketing people – they can all lead us to make badly informed, if not incorrect, decisions.

We all know that sometimes what appears on the surface is not the full picture. They say the devil is in the detail and, given the cost and value of real estate, this is something no one wants to get wrong.

In this chapter, I am going to share a very practical, efficient and simple process which will enable you to benchmark any real estate asset, so that you fully understand how much value it offers you.

KEY ELEMENTS OF EVERY INVESTMENT DECISION

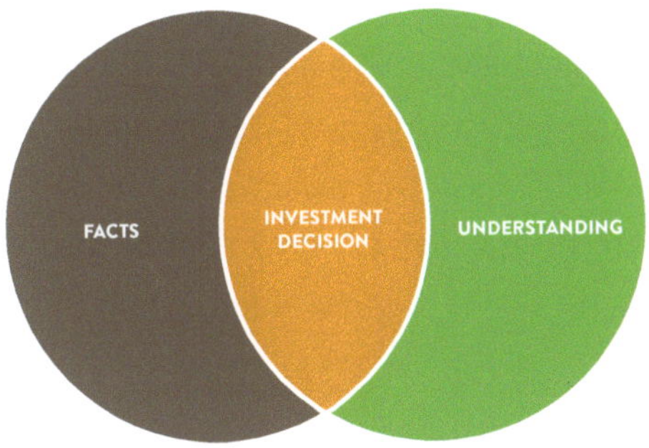

FACTS AND UNDERSTANDING

The first element is the facts which you can list in 'fact sheet' form. This will cover static information such as size, price, leasable area, view and so on. Basically, it is often the set of information you see on all property ads and brochures. We can't, however, make accurate decisions based simply on a fact sheet, which is where the importance of the second element comes into play.

This is an in-depth understanding of the features and the benefits of the product compared to two or three other similar products, viewed through the perspective of all the macro and micro fundamentals of the marketplace. To achieve this understanding, I have come up with a very simple, but accurate, realistic and effective process I call CAAD: comparison, analysis, assessment and decision.

I apply CAAD to every project before I make any personal or institutional investment decision as well as before presenting any kind of real estate investment advice to my clients.

I will now share the CAAD process with you in detail – and explain how you can apply it to your own investments. I will also share with you a practical application or template you can use by yourself, whether you are a savvy real estate investor or simply a homebuyer. In either capacity, you still – naturally – want to get the best possible value for every dollar you spend.

First of all, though, you need to remember that the emotional side of making a purchasing decision is a factor which often makes investors vulnerable. How? Because they take their attention away from the facts and figures which matter the most. Not only that, they also distract their attention onto those "smiley happy lifestyle" marketing images, which may or may not be a genuine reflection of the realities.

Whether you are buying a real estate asset to live in or for investment, in either case you have to follow exactly the same process: grounded in analysing numbers, facts and the fundamentals of the market, i.e. trends, data and so on.

The difference between the two sorts of purchaser lies in their key preferences. End users (people buying a home to live in) first need to choose a few projects which tick all their living requirements, then compare them to see which one offers them the best value for their money.

Investors, meanwhile, often focus only on numbers and commercial viability without any distinct or definite preferences for locations, layouts or other set of criteria.

I am now going to show a way of examining a set of the most important features and benefits through rational and unbiased comparative criteria to lead you to a quantifiable conclusion and the right investment decision.

THE CAAD PROCESS

The CAAD process comprises two main steps:

The first is COMPARISON. The comparison table on the next page enables you to read how all the features and benefits of one project are benchmarked against the other one or more projects. Having all these facts set out on one sheet gives you a very clear all-round understanding of the value you are getting out of each project.

The second is ANALYSIS, ASSESSMENT, DECISION. Analysis of each project enables you to assess which one offers you the best value in light of your needs and preferences, so you can make the right investment decision.

The second table uses typical names and numbers as an example; what is important here is how it works – which we will go into in greater detail later.

REAL ESTATE VALUE IS MEASURED BY THE INCH – NOT JUST THE PHYSICAL INCH, BUT ALSO FROM THE VIEW THROUGH THE WINDOWS TO THE INTERIOR LAYOUT AND THE QUALITY OF THE FITTINGS.

THE COMPARISON TABLE

THIS COMPARISON CRITERIA IS FOR XXXX APARTMENT/VILLA	PROJECT 1	PROJECT 2	PROJECT 3
Price per sq. ft. for the MOST attractive unit			
Price per sq. ft. for the LEAST attractive unit			
Total Price for the MOST attractive unit			
Total Price for the LEAST attractive unit			
Total unit size			
Balcony size			
Internal area size			
Supply and demand			
Direct access to beach/metro/mall/etc.			
The differentiator			
Data and Statistics			
Annual service charges			
Expected annual rent			
Others (tenanted, ready, time left to completion, development quality, etc.			

COMPARISON CRITERIA	THE RESIDENCES	OLD TOWN	CITY WALK
Price per sq. ft. for the MOST attractive unit (view and layout)	3,000 – 3,300 AED	2,500 – 2,800 AED	1,900 – 2,200 AED
Price per sq. ft. for the LEAST attractive unit (view and layout)	1,800 – 2,000 AED	1,600 – 1,800 AED	1,500 – 1,700 AED
Supply and demand (for associated buildings)	Modern high rise – strong demand vs strong supply	Moroccan-style; small windows and less natural light. Low supply vs low demand. (Low historical price appreciation as compared to other Downtown projects)	Modern low rise – extremely limited supply vs a very high demand. (The only low rise in prime Dubai and the first freehold in Jumeirah area)
Density of master community	Part of Downtown which consists of 6,000-plus similar range of ready apartments; and more to come	Although it is the only low-rise project in Downtown; yet it is still centrally located in a master community of 7,000-plus units	Part of a unique concept of ready 34 low-rise modern buildings; having a total of only 1,700 apartments with a minimal projection of similar leverage to happen
Ongoing maintenance quality and master developer's reputation	Best in Dubai	Best in Dubai	Best in Dubai and the "Future Image of the Country"
Product finishing (rating out of 10) "within the same class of apartments and price range"	9 out of 10 (depending on which building)	7 out of 10	8 out of 10
Location and accessibility	Downtown: access to Burj Khalifa, the Fountain, Dubai Mall	Downtown: access to MBR Boulevard, Dubai Mall, Business Bay	Jumeirah: access to Downtown as a whole, Four Seasons Hotel, La Mer Beach, Box Park, Bvlgari Hotel, Nikki Beach
Anticipated price appreciation	Already completed – fluctuates with market index	Already completed – fluctuates with market index	Upon full maturity of the project, completion of retail establishments and entertainment destinations, prices will skyrocket
Project age	9 years	10 years	Brand new (investors don't pay premium and end users are the first to occupy their homes)
Payment plan and financing	No payment plan – possibility of mortgage	No payment plan – possibility of mortgage	Post-handover payment plan on 24 months with a financing incentive from all Dubai banks
Master community	Popular touristic destination	Popular touristic destination	Unique cosmopolitan community with first time ever concepts

FROM THIS, WE CAN CONCLUDE THAT:
City Walk average prices are 22 per cent less compared to a combined Downtown average.
City Walk urban density is 73 per cent less compared to Downtown.
City Walk price appreciation is granted while that of Downtown is uncertain.
City Walk demand is unpredictably high vs a continuous Downtown supply.
City Walk accessibility is much effortless compared to Downtown.
City Walk is ten years younger than Downtown.

FIG. 15: An example of a comparison table showing the projects, the comparison criteria, the information or data, as well as the conclusions drawn from this table.

As you read further, you will learn how to apply this process to any project in any market. Understanding it might initially take a bit of concentration, but it will soon make complete sense to you, and once you fully grasp this process, you will find it easy to use.

HOW TO APPLY THE CAAD PROCESS

STEP ONE: COMPARISON

The comparison table comprises of three main elements:

- Projects
- Comparison Criteria
- Information or data

PROJECTS

Here is how you can choose the projects you want to include in your comparison table. If you are interested in Project X, think about one, two or even three other most competitive and comparable projects that you might also be interested in, because they also offer more or less the same value. Ask yourself:

- If project X was no longer available or did not exist, what would be your project Y?
- If project Y was not there, what would be your project Z?
- If you had a slightly lower budget, what other projects would you consider?
- If you have a slightly higher budget, what other projects would you consider?

COMPARISON CRITERIA

This is the set of criteria you will use to qualify the value each of the projects offers in light of exactly the same criteria. For instance, if it is the price per square foot, then which of the three projects offers the best price, or if it is the total price, which one offers the best total price, and so on.

In order for you to arrive at an accurate and correct conclusion, you have to ensure that you don't miss any important piece of information in your comparison table. So how do you arrive at the right set of criteria? There are no set rules, but there are two things that will help you, without being biased towards one project or another:

- The most common comparison criteria.
- The thought process you need to follow.

THE MOST COMMON COMPARISON CRITERIA COMPRISE:		
(1) Basic aspects	(2) Aspects that make a project superior to other similar projects	(3) Aspects which, conversely, could be a major disadvantage

The thought process you need to follow, which will help you to compare one master community to another, one project to another or even one particular real estate unit to another, within the same project or across different projects.

I'm sharing some tips on the thought process which will help you create your own criteria, based on the nature of the comparable assets you choose. You need to consider the following questions, in light of the three or more projects that you have in mind for comparison:

- What are the main features?
- What are the main benefits?
- What are the main pros and cons?
- What are the main differentiators of each project?
- Why would an end-user love or hate the project or the real estate unit?
- You can also include criteria based on:
  - — How many units are sold on the market within a particular period of time?

- The negative or positive price difference between the current price and the original price of the property at the time it was sold by the developer?
- The total number of available properties in each project.

MARKET COMPARISON (THE COMPARISON CRITERIA)

How to choose different aspects for comparison criteria

THE BASIC ASPECT

Price per sq. ft. for the MOST attractive unit

Price per sq. ft. for the LEAST attractive unit

Total Price for the MOST attractive unit

Total Price for the LEAST attractive unit

Unit size

Balcony ratio out of the total unit size

Supply and demand

Is it the type of property that makes it undersupplied?

Is it the price?

Is it the master community?

Is it the location?

Is it one of the elements of the master community?

ASPECTS THAT MAKE THE PROJECT SUPERIOR

What are the components that set any of the three projects at a different level from an investment point of view?

Is it the project age? Is it the layout? Is it the prestigious neighbourhood?

Is it the payment plan?

Does it have extra rooms?

Is the plot bigger in size?

Is it the low density?

Is it the large common recreation or green area?

ASPECTS THAT ARE A MAJOR DISADVANTAGE TO YOUR PROJECT

What could be deemed as a disadvantage for any of the projects?

Example, Project X does not offer any facilities (could be deemed as a disadvantage). Small sizes, poor accessibility, no proper lobby, a new developer with no track record, etc.

FIG. 16: An example showing the most common aspects of the comparison criteria.

Answering these questions will enable you to create a suitable set of criteria that you can then use to assess your comparable projects.

INFORMATION OR DATA

Now that I've explained the first two elements of the comparison table – the comparable projects and the comparison criteria – we move on to the third: the 'required information' you need to complete. In essence, the first two elements are what inspires the questions which need to be answered to obtain this information.

Some questions are related to price, some to size. Answers to these should be easy for you to find as most of them are part of the project fact sheet defined earlier in this chapter, but there are other questions which might require you to speak to different experts and look at reliable sources of market data.

These other questions may be related to market data, historical price trends, project age, property physical conditions and so on. You will need to focus carefully, and it may require some extra effort, as you could well have to ask different experts the same questions, then analyse the different answers and assess which answer is the most accurate.

Finally, we use this collected information to populate the comparison table.

*****

We have now looked at the three elements which make up the comparison table: Projects, Comparison Criteria and Information or Data. If you complete these three elements properly, you will have a perfect comparison table, which will enable you to see each of the projects you have chosen to compare, in the light of each of the criteria that matter to you.

For instance, if you were looking at the price per square foot for Project X, you would also see what it is in Projects Y and Z.

Having all this information collected together in the right sequence on a single page and in a single table enables you to form a very good and clear understanding of each of the projects you are comparing – and shows you which one could provide the best value for money, taking into consideration all of your personal criteria.

STEP TWO: ANALYSIS, ASSESSMENT, DECISION

As stated previously, the second section of the CAAD process is taking the Comparison table and using Analysis and Assessment to arrive at your investment Decision.

Let's look at how you can derive the correct conclusion from the details you gather in the comparison table. This is achieved through three simple stages.

- **Compare:** Look at the comparison table and study it thoroughly.
- **Analyse:** Take note of any major differences between your original chosen project and the other comparable projects, in terms of the criteria you are using.
- **Assess:** Quantify, in numbers, each of the differences you spotted in the first and second stages.

The differences you see may reveal positive or negative results about your original chosen project. For instance, looking at the first stage, it might tick the box for the luxury recreation areas and facilities the other two projects have. However, with fewer facilities and recreation areas in a project, the annual service charges and the overall maintenance of that project will cost a lot less than the other projects. So, if you are seeking rental income at a lesser cost, maybe this project will generate higher rental income for you.

That's why during the first *comparison stage*, you need to look at criteria which might reveal extreme differences between the original project of your interest and the other comparable projects in the second *analysis stage*.

To give you another example, maybe you'll see that the price per square foot of the original project is higher than the price per square foot in the other two projects. However, it offers a much bigger internal area, whereas the other two projects offer much larger outside areas like a terrace or garden area, which in many ways justifies the higher price per square foot of the original project.

The third *assessment stage* is absolutely critical, in order to quantify in numbers each of the differences you spotted in the second stage.

For example, let's assume that you are comparing two villas. The first villa is priced at 12 million dollars, the second at 10 million. Although both villas have exactly the same leasable/liveable or internal area, the first villa is a corner plot or is constructed on a corner plot that offers an extra 6,000 square feet. So, instead of coming to a conclusion purely through stage one, you've spotted this major difference in stage two, and so in stage three, we want to quantify the difference and boil it down to pure numbers – rationally, not emotionally.

In conclusion, although villa number one is priced at 2 million more than villa number two, you need to note that villa number one offers an extra 6,000 square feet. When you look at a rate per square foot of 600 dollars, the total price for the 6,000 square feet is 3.6 million, which means you're not actually paying 2 million extra, but saving 1.6 million in the form of 6,000 extra square feet, and you are getting a prime corner plot.

To give you another example...

Let's assume that we are comparing three projects. Project number one does not have a swimming pool and recreational areas, but projects two and three do. However, projects numbers two and three also have extra service charges for the additional amenities.

The annual service charge for project number one is only 8 dollars per square foot, while the annual service charges for projects number two and three amounts to 13 dollars per square foot – almost double. So, if you are renting out these units, although you are paying higher annual service charges in projects two and three, you will also achieve 50 dollars more per square foot as annual rental income due to offering more facilities such as swimming pools.

	PROJECT 1	PROJECT 2	PROJECT 3
Swimming Pool	NO	YES	YES
Annual service charges (cost)	$ 8.00	$ 13.00	$ 13.00
Annual rental income per sq. ft.	$ 100.00	$ 150.00	$ 150.00
Net annual rental income per sq. ft.	$ 92.00	$ 137.00	$ 137.00
Purchase price per sq. ft.	$ 800.00	$ 900.00	$ 900.00
Gross ROI on rent	13%	17%	17%
Net ROI on rent	12%	15%	15%

FIG. 17: An example of a comparison chart.

In conclusion, in project one you are paying 5 dollars per square foot extra as compared to projects two and three, but you are getting extra 50 dollars as rental income per square foot as rental income. So, project number two and three offers approximately 30 per cent higher net rental income as compared to project one (15 per cent net rental income for project two and three as compared to only 12 per cent net rental income for project one).

So, in essence, stage two is looking at – analysing – all the significant differences. Then stage three is all about weighing – assessing – the pros and cons in the most quantifiable way. Arriving at the right decision boils down to numbers. By applying this process throughout your comparison, you will be able to identify which of the projects you are looking at offers the best value for your money.

Please note that the data and statistics mentioned in the previous chapter are an integral part of the CAAD process. So, you still need to compare the different data and statistics related criteria for each of the three projects and see which one has the best value.

Please don't be intimidated by the amount of information in the tables and the process. To remind you about what I mentioned earlier, CAAD is just a written and professional version of the process, which in some form, most of us follow one way or another when we buy any product. Comparing different products with the aim of finding out which offers the best value is an integral part of any buying decision – and CAAD makes it easy for you to do exactly that when thinking about your real estate investment.

However, there are some things you need to look out for. You might be wondering why I mentioned the price per square foot for the most attractive unit and the price per square foot for the least attractive unit as well as the same for the total price as part of the criteria in the comparison table. It's simply because, as I previously mentioned, sometimes one of the variables may look very attractive, but in reality, it is not.

Let me give you a typical example: You might not notice it at first, but the balcony, garden or outdoor area of any apartment, villa, townhouse or penthouse can drastically affect the price or the average price per square foot for the internal area. This is because, for obvious reasons, the construction cost of the internal area is set at many multiples of the construction cost of the balcony or garden – hence, the sales price is different.

For instance, you might be looking at one specific area and see that the average price per square foot is around 1500 dollars per square foot. Then all of a sudden you see one property advertised at 900 dollars per square foot on the same exact location or project. It feels like you've found the platinum deal you've been looking for. But when you go into the details, you might see that one of the possible reasons for this massive difference is the fact that the apartment priced at 900 per square foot has a much larger balcony or garden to internal area ratio. In other words, it offers a much lower internal area as compared to the standard apartments.

Here's another example: You might be looking at a one-bedroom apartment advertised at 1.2 million, but then in the project next to it, you see there is also a one-bedroom apartment advertised at 900,000. If one of the main reasons for the price difference is the size, you are most likely to be getting a much bigger apartment at 1.2 million.

When you see all this information in the right sequence in one single comparison table, you be able to identify, analyse and assess your options clearly. All you need to think about will be readily available, so you can make a fully informed decision.

Next, in the final chapter, I'll tell you about one of the most important things you need to do as a part of your real estate investment – being able to negotiate and close a good deal.

CHAPTER 11

HOW TO NEGOTIATE AND CLOSE A GOOD DEAL

KEY POINTS:

- SIX TIPS TO HELP YOU NEGOTIATE THE BEST DEAL
  - **TIP ONE: NEGOTIATE THROUGH A PROFESSIONAL MIDDLE PARTY**
  - **TIP TWO: FACTORS TO CONSIDER DURING NEGOTIATIONS**
    - — Factor One: Price
    - — Factor Two: Payment
    - — Factor Three: Fees
    - — Factor Four: Lead Time
    - — Factor Five: Rights and Liabilities
    - — Factor Six: Keys
    - — Factor Seven: Property Status
    - — Factor Eight: Parking
    - — Factor Nine: Default Clauses
    - — Factor Ten: Legal and Force Majeure
  - **TIP THREE: BUYING PROPERTIES ON THE PRIMARY MARKET**
    - — Payment Terms
    - — Annual Service Charge
    - — Completion Date
    - — Key Handover Date
    - — Property Inspection
    - — Schedule of Finishing Materials
  - **TIP FOUR: CLOSURE - DON'T HESITATE AND LOSE THE DEAL**
  - **TIP FIVE: WELL-DEFINED LEGALITIES**
    - — Why Employ a Legal Consultant?
    - — When to Engage a Legal Consultant?
    - — What Does the Lawyer Do?
    - — How Can a Lawyer Help You?
  - **TIP SIX: THINGS TO KEEP IN MIND WHEN NEGOTIATING LEASES**
- THE FINAL WORD

"The only way to find out is to enter into a negotiation process."

– Nancy Tallman

Now that you have seen how to decide which property, or properties you are going to invest in, we move onto one of the most important elements in any business, including real estate – negotiating and closing the deal.

I'm sure you're already aware of classic negotiation skills and tactics such as: don't play all your cards at once, don't show excitement or become emotional, don't take it all personally and so on.

However, negotiating real estate transactions requires a wider understanding not just of the immediate implications of the transaction – but also of your long-term interests in the market, including but not limited to commercial and legal aspects, which many real estate investors overlook as considerations.

I would now like to share some valuable tips on how you should conduct your deals.

SIX TIPS TO HELP YOU NEGOTIATE THE BEST DEAL

TIP ONE: NEGOTIATE THROUGH A PROFESSIONAL MIDDLE PARTY

It's better not to negotiate directly, or face to face. Whether you are a buyer, seller, landlord or a tenant, it is always better to negotiate through a professional middle party, carefully chosen and fully briefed to work towards your best interests. This is because, if you get into direct negotiation, you may be negatively affected by:

- **Lack of time to think.** Sometimes, if you are negotiating with a well-seasoned and experienced party, you might be cornered into making an on-the-spot decision. Not a good idea. With a middle party acting as a go-between, it is always easier to ask for more time to consider your options.

START YOUR REAL ESTATE JOURNEY WITH THE RIGHT REAL ESTATE CONSULTANT BY YOUR SIDE – YOUR KNOWLEDGE PARTNER – FOR THEIR GUIDANCE AND NEGOTIATION SKILLS.

- **Getting personal.** Sometimes egos get in the way when two financially capable parties meet without having any background knowledge about each other or any prior dealings. Remember, it's about the deal, not personalities – so leave it to a professional.

Also, you might also miss out on these benefits:

- **Being able to "test the waters".** A middle party can ask candid questions you might not be able to and then pass on hints and clues about the position of the other party and how motivated they are to buy or to sell.
- **Flexibility.** By working through a middle party, you maintain a certain level of flexibility, so you won't become side-tracked in your negotiations. Your representative can always ask to be allowed to get back to you and come up with an alternative suggestion or offer, and so can the other negotiating party.
- **Expertise and experience.** An experienced middle party is likely to achieve better results for you, as long as you explain to them what you want to achieve, and you mandate them to go ahead with it.

As I have said in earlier chapters, it is essential to start your real estate search by having the right real estate consultant by your side – your knowledge partner.

This is for two reasons: to guide you and influence your decision-making processes, as well as to negotiate on your behalf to get you the best deal. Their market knowledge and experience will prove invaluable, because, without it, even the best negotiator may end up with a bad deal.

TIP TWO: FACTORS TO CONSIDER DURING NEGOTIATIONS

FACTOR ONE: PRICE

Get the price right by ensuring your negotiation strategy reflects these factors:

- Understanding the motives of the seller.
- Understanding the level of demand in the market for

this unit or project, so you can define the time frame available for negotiation, without risking losing the deal to another buyer.

- Understanding the market data.
- All the information you have gathered during the CAAD process.

FACTOR TWO: PAYMENT

1. Type of payment. Do you have a preferred payment method? How can you use it? It could be a different currency or bitcoin, etc.

Depending on the market, exchanging British pounds to UAE dirhams, for instance, can sometimes be an advantage or a disadvantage. So, negotiating a time frame to make the payment when rates best suit your interests can make a real difference.

2. Down payment and security. How much is required as a deposit and who is the escrow agent to hold that payment? Is it secured?

FACTOR THREE: FEES

Paying the brokerage commission and the other related fees. Who will pay the brokerage commission and the other related fees, if there are any? You have to be aware of the market norms and follow them accordingly.

FACTOR FOUR: LEAD TIME

Lead time to conclude the transaction and extensions. Do you need to state a fixed time frame to conclude the transaction or to allow for an extension to the contract – in case, for any reason, it takes you longer to make all the necessary arrangements to finalise the transaction?

FACTOR FIVE: RIGHTS AND LIABILITIES

Past, current and future asset rights and liabilities. All rights and obligations should only be transferred to the new buyer once the full ownership is transferred to the buyer or a sales and purchase agreement is duly signed by both parties.

Why is this? Well, questions like this might arise: *If the property is rented, who gets the rent until the transfer of the ownership is completed? How is that process going to happen?*

FACTOR SIX: KEYS

Handover of keys and other access devices. Establish a time frame and method for this, if required.

FACTOR SEVEN: PROPERTY STATUS

Property status upon finalising the transaction. Are you buying on an "as seen" basis? Or does the seller have to rectify or complete any parts of the property?

FACTOR EIGHT: PARKING

Parking spaces. Ownership of the parking should be included too, where applicable.

FACTOR NINE: DEFAULT CLAUSES

Default and compensation clauses for both parties. In case of default by the buyer or the seller, what is the pre-defined and agreed course of action? Make sure it is all well defined in your contract of sales and purchase.

FACTOR TEN: LEGAL AND FORCE MAJEURE

1. Legal jurisdiction. In case of any legal conflict, what is the pre-defined and agreed legal jurisdiction process?

2. Force majeure. In case of any force majeure, what are the rights and obligations of both parties?

Apart from these ten factors, if you are a seller, here are some additional factors to consider during negotiating a sale for your property:

- **Understanding your buyers:** Why are they buying your property? Are they under any time pressure?

- **Understanding their alternative options:** What other options (i.e. other properties on the market) do your buyers have, how much do they cost and how well do they answer their needs? For example, you may have a buyer who wants to move in before the school year starts for his/her kids. There are other options in the market similar to yours, but they will only be ready two months after the school start date. This can give you the upper hand when negotiating.
- **Keeping your selling motives to yourself:** You don't have to reveal your reason for selling. Doing so might work against you.

TIP THREE: BUYING PROPERTIES ON THE PRIMARY MARKET

When buying properties on the primary market, i.e. first buyer from the real estate developer, remember that if you decide to sell the property before completion, the new buyer will most likely inherit the same sales and purchase agreement that you signed. Which means, negotiating and signing a well-structured contract is a very critical step even if you decide to sell the property before or after completion. Here is your top negotiation checklist:

PAYMENT TERMS

- In one payment? Or via multiple instalments? How important is that for you on your list of priorities?
- If you are paying through instalments, what are the penalties and consequences if you default?
- Are you ready to pay a higher price in order to secure your preferred payment terms (if you are after a comfortable longer-term payment plan as opposed to a one-time payment or short-term payment plan)?

ANNUAL SERVICE CHARGE

- How much is it?
- When does it start? Is it when you receive notice for handover, when you get the key, or when you have the

key and checked the apartment, and the developer has rectified any possible defects you might identify?
- What does it cover?

COMPLETION DATE

- When is the completion date?
- What compensation do you receive if there is a delay?

KEY HANDOVER DATE

- What is the definition of key handover day?
- Are there any charges associated with it?

PROPERTY INSPECTION

- What are your rights in terms of inspecting the property with a professional snagging company?
- When will the developer rectify any faults and snags identified?

SCHEDULE OF FINISHING MATERIALS

- Read the schedule of finishings (materials used to build) and cross-check it with the actual materials once the property is due for handover through a professional property inspection expert.
- How much can the developer change without your consent as a property owner or investor?

TIP FOUR: CLOSURE – DON'T HESITATE AND LOSE THE DEAL

Remember... you don't have to milk the negotiations for every last penny, cent or fil. Sometimes, trying to achieve one tiny bit of extra gain exposes you to the risk of losing a big chunk of profit, by missing out on buying a well-priced property, or selling or renting out at a decent price.

Whether you are a buyer, seller or landlord, if you've arrived at a deal that ticks all your main boxes and aims, sign and seal it without overthinking it and without any further hesitation. Negotiating for minimal extra benefits

NEGOTIATING REAL ESTATE TRANSACTIONS REQUIRES A WIDER UNDERSTANDING NOT JUST OF THE IMMEDIATE IMPLICATIONS OF THE TRANSACTION – BUT ALSO OF YOUR LONG-TERM INTERESTS IN THE MARKET

can prolong the process – and during that time, the other party might get a better deal elsewhere.

Remember… if you have left no stone unturned during the CAAD process and you conducted it correctly, you are more likely to make a very profitable deal as a buyer, seller or landlord.

TIP FIVE: WELL-DEFINED LEGALITIES

Once you have finalised the negotiation of the commercial terms of the transaction, it is time to ensure that all the agreed commercial terms are well defined in a legal context. Here are some of the reasons why and when you need to employ a specialist legal consultant, and what they will do for you:

WHY EMPLOY A LEGAL CONSULTANT?

Getting the deal right is not just about the commercial aspects, the legal side is vitally important too. Okay, you have negotiated correctly and successfully, and you have agreed on the best price, terms and conditions related to your transaction.

However, it's not all done yet. The next step is to check the legal side of the transaction. This is essential, but it is where I have seen many investors become confused as they don't have sufficient legal knowledge. I always advise investors to have a legal consultant with them to check all the contracts, paperwork and formalities related to the transaction. I also strongly suggest that they maintain the correct balance between the commercial and legal sides of the deal.

WHEN TO ENGAGE A LEGAL CONSULTANT?

Basically, the right time to engage a legal consultant to check your transaction is after you have finalised your commercial negotiation with the other party(ies) involved and agreed on the commercials in terms of price, method of payment, the payment plan, status of the property, desired ownership structure and so on.

Once all this is done, you are ready to hire a professional real estate lawyer to ensure that all the commercial terms agreed with the seller and/or broker are in compliance with the relevant laws and regulations. More importantly, you need to be sure that you are in possession of the required guarantees and warranties to protect and enforce your rights as per the agreed terms, should the other party default on delivering their obligations.

WHAT DOES THE LAWYER DO?

Investors sometimes simply find the right property and pass the rest of the work to a lawyer. But of course, the lawyer's interest and expertise lie in the legal aspects. They are not always the best people to handle commercial arrangements, so you – as the investor – must take responsibility for finalising the commercial terms, and then get a legal opinion, as a lawyer might see something that might be relevant in the future, or immediately, which is worth flagging to you. It is then up to you to decide the way forward. You are responsible for your own investment decisions.

HOW CAN A LAWYER HELP YOU?

Here are some examples of how a lawyer can ensure the legalities of a transaction after you agree on the commercial terms:

1. If you are buying a property with guaranteed rental income, a specialist lawyer will look into the guarantor and double check their solvency along with other important factors. If you have agreed with the seller that there is a rental guarantee, but it turns out that the guarantor is not solvent, then the guarantee is actually completely worthless.

2. If you're buying a tenanted property and you have agreed with the seller that the rent will start coming to you from the date of transfer, your lawyer will verify the tenancy contract with the tenant, and the current and future obligations and rights stated on the tenancy contract. He will then flag up any concerns, such as:

- Has the landlord or seller been paid the rent in full? If they have, the seller has to refund the rent starting from the ownership transfer date.
- Are there any post-dated rent cheques under the current landlords' name? How and when those cheques are going to be replaced with new checks under your name as the buyer and future landlord?
- Any other concerns the lawyer might identify.

3. If you are buying a property under construction, the lawyer will examine aspects such as:

- When will the property be handed over to you?
- What are the completion milestones linked to your payment plan?
- What are the obligations of the developer in case of a delay in handover, or of default?
- What are the rights of the developer in case you were late in making a due payment?

There are endless other potential scenarios when you are making a real estate transaction – that is why having a lawyer in place to check your contract is absolutely essential.

TIP SIX: THINGS TO KEEP IN MIND WHEN NEGOTIATING LEASES

Here are some points to negotiate if you are a landlord leasing out property:

- Rental price
- Form of payment
- Down payment and security deposit
- Other related fees
- Utility account registration
- Preventative maintenance visits
- Periodic access to the property
- Maintenance

- Property management
- Contract renewal
- Termination notice
- Penalties in case of payment defaults
- Handover of keys and other access devices
- Property status upon key handover/move-in form
- Parking spaces
- Legal jurisdiction
- Force majeure

*****

THE FINAL WORD

In order for you to fully utilise this information during negotiating your next transaction or deal, make sure that you create your own personalised checklist based on these six tips, as you see applicable. Choose what you deem appropriate to the scenario of your deal, and then go ahead and tick them one by one. By the time they are all ticked, you are likely to have struck the best deal while all your short- and long-term rights are legally protected.

Last but not least, ensure that you are getting the best out of your deal. But remember the old saying, "Don't spend a dollar to save a dime". The same way this analogy applies to money, it also applies to the time and effort you invest in any kind of negotiation.

EPILOGUE

WHERE NEXT?

PUTTING YOUR KNOWLEDGE INTO ACTION

Thank you for taking the time to read my book. I sincerely hope that I have covered all the topics necessary for you to make a sound investment, whether you already have some real estate experience or have none at all. I have tried my best to help guide you through each step, identifying and avoiding red flags, identifying the right opportunity, and successfully negotiating your way towards a profitable investment.

The thought I would like to leave you with is that, no matter how much we follow the facts and statistics and the fundamentals and science of buying real estate, it is naturally impossible to isolate ourselves from our emotions and instincts. But, as long as these aspects are not your key motivators and the core of your decision-making process remains grounded in the correct fundamentals, you will always be able to minimise risk and maximise your chances of profit.

PRACTICE MAKES PERFECT

It is crucial to be aware that there is always a starting point, and from there forward, 'deliberate practice' makes perfect. You should distinguish 'deliberate practice' from 'practice', which could be defined as the repetition of a skill until it becomes almost second nature. Deliberate practice, however, is practice with unwavering attention and aim to constantly improve, with a clear awareness of what components deliver the best results and knowing how to continue improving them.

In my experience from investing for myself, advising and guiding investors as well as being blessed to have the opportunity to train thousands of real estate agents, the more you put into action the guidelines I have outlined in this book, the more benefits you can reap. The good news is that, from the very start, following the processes I have explained will minimise your risk in every way – and as time goes by – will lead you to better outcomes.

As you progress, try and feed off the confidence in your decision-making which you will gain by diligently following the investment guidance provided. The process is not complicated, and the approach and fundamental steps here apply to markets around the world. It is, in a way, a reflection of any and every purchase you make on a daily basis – with the additional factor of having more data and findings to read, understand and analyse before making that purchase. In time, you will start to feel at ease about your decision to invest in real estate as you have carried out the correct processes that enable you to make a well-informed decision.

Of course, following this approach does not mean that you invest in a property that you don't like. You need to identify the best among the properties you like and establish the critical findings explained in this book to ensure that you are making the right choice, in every way.

SUCCESS IN REAL ESTATE

I urge you to be among the top 1 per cent of successful people: those who take the knowledge they have gained and put it into practice.

To further help you on your way, I would like to extend my commitment to providing you with the required resources and support that you need for the most profitable real estate investment ventures. Please don't hesitate to connect with me via our website or social media pages (addresses on the following page). You can also visit our website to access a wide range of real estate opportunities.

You can also find the link for our corporate brochure and our wide spectrum of services, including sales, leasing, property management, property engineered snagging and inspection, real estate development management and investment advisory, holiday homes, interior design and real estate mortgages for individual and institutional real estate investors and homebuyers. Look out, too, for announcements about our new accredited real estate academy.

I look forward to hearing from you about your success in real estate investment.

Please feel free to contact me for any advice or guidance you might want or need, at:

- Instagram: @firas_al_msaddi
- Twitter: @ceofamprop
- TikTok: @firasalmsaddi
- LinkedIn: Firas Al Msaddi
- Company website: www.famproperties.com

TAKING UP A CAREER IN REAL ESTATE INVESTMENT

By now, some of you might even be considering real estate investments as a possible profession and long-term career. To help you get started on the right foot, I will leave you with some simple guidelines.

SOME ESSENTIAL CONSIDERATIONS

To start with, here is the most basic principle of making money:

We have talked about the importance of practice and gaining experience: your experience in a business often defines how successful you are in that business, and that translates into how much money you make. Only successful businesses make money, of course.

So, when everything revolves around experience, which is in simple terms 'practised knowledge', the best organisations to join are those with a systematic learning and development infrastructure, starting with onboarding and through to providing ongoing knowledge and an efficient platform to practice. You also need to join an ambitious organisation that offers serious personal and career growth opportunities – you can only grow so much, even in a successful organisation, if it prefers to remain at a boutique size.

GAIN KNOWLEDGE → PRACTICE YOUR KNOWLEDGE = EXPERIENCE

THE BEST KNOWLEDGE → PRACTICE THE MOST = THE BEST EXPERIENCE

THE MOST EXPERIENCED ALWAYS DO BEST IN BUSINESS AND OUTPERFORMS COMPETITORS

THE BEST IN BUSINESS ALWAYS EARNS THE MOST MONEY

So, if you are considering taking up a job as a real estate agent, the first and most essential investment you can make is spending significant time and energy on finding the right organisation: one which offers you a genuine opportunity for growth.

YOUR CHOSEN ORGANISATION SHOULD...

- Be a totally client-centric company. For any company to provide excellent client experience, it has to start by treating its employees right and providing its employees with all required training, knowledge, experience and effective resources, not to mention providing employees with fair income and career growth opportunities. Check out client reviews on Google and other sites that offer feedback. The future of business is owned by client-centric organisations. As an employee, never expect much from organisations that are not client-centric.
- Offer you room to grow and develop, providing a qualified source of knowledge and personal training, along with an environment and a practical platform which enables employees to implement what they are learning within their daily tasks.
- Recognise its responsibility to provide employee support as early as at the on-boarding stage and until the employee is ready to operate successfully with minimum supervision.
- Be stable and well-established, with good leadership and a proven track record.

In the right organisation, you will gain the experience required to build a lifetime career or lead a higher quality of life through improved job satisfaction. I am a passionate believer in the importance of sharing knowledge and experience which adds value for other people, most especially for my team.

As a results-orientated entrepreneur with a track record of building successful businesses from the ground up, I am convinced that it is one of the most important qualities a leader must have. I truly believe that many employees are victims of their own decision to join and stay with organisations that are simply not the right fit for them. The reasons for this could be because the organisation:

- Does not share their values.
- Does not invest in quality leadership and management. Instead, it has leaders who fail to motivate, inspire and lead by example and experience, and therefore don't help their team be fulfilled and achieve their career goals.
- Does not have the right corporate structure in place, so career progression is unclear.
- Does not invest in long-term plans and initiatives so it does not provide job security.
- Does not realise the importance of developing employee skills and training.
- Does not invest in strategy to robustly answer the challenges of ever-changing markets.

HOW DO YOU CHOOSE THE RIGHT ORGANISATION?

Do your research, compare different companies in the light of your ideal criteria and what and where you want to reach in your career. Taking real care when choosing the right organisation to join is absolutely crucial because:

- **It can fast track your success, set you back or put you off track.** Whichever career path you set out on and whatever company you choose, it will dictate to where your career leads. Your first company will define the way you see your industry and your career. It's make or break – you make the wrong decision, and you delay your success. It is that simple, with no turning back or excuses.
- **You have to be practical and objective.** The best company for you will always be the one that will inspire and motivate you to last the course through thick and thin. Different people are inspired by different things

and draw strength from different motives – choose what naturally drives you to always strive to do better.

- **Track record is important.** In this generation where almost everyone is being pushed to open their own businesses, with the false impression that it's the only way to "get rich quick", most businesses tend to fail. That's because many "wannabe" entrepreneurs are eager to earn more, but not willing to work more, invest more and take bolder risks. The ideal company for you will be headed by a leader who is a strategist and has a proven track record. Someone who has been through the ups and downs of the market, and who can sell regardless of the stage in the market cycle: someone who has "seen it all" and has worked successfully at every stage while they continue to be eager to acquire new knowledge and learn even more. The captain always steers the ship – so make sure you choose the right captain.
- **Serious growth.** The best organisations are led by people who never cease to grow and learn. People who always reaches out to new horizons and can turn an idea into good business. You should join a company that will provide you with plenty of opportunities to progress. This is only possible if the company itself invests the right resources to secure its place in the market and to grow its business, always moving forward or upward. The history of the company speaks volumes of where it's heading to.

fäm® Properties

At fäm Properties, we provide you with the best industry knowledge and the platform to practice what you learn, so you can gain the required experience to win big in real estate.

If you are interested, please feel free to contact us at:

- Company website: www.famproperties.com
- Instagram: @famcareers
- LinkedIn: fäm Properties Dubai

If you fully and carefully follow this advice you could be on the way to a rewarding and fulfilling career as a real estate professional.

www.ingramcontent.com/pod-product-compliance
Lightning Source LLC
LaVergne TN
LVHW071244210926
848486LV00008B/342
9781860635434